Extreme

Intuitive

Makeover

55 Keys to Health, Wealth,
and Happiness

Dear Dawn,
Many Blessings
as you share your
intuitive gifts
Anne

Extreme

Intuitive

Makeover

55 Keys to Health, Wealth, and Happiness

Anne Deidre

MAVEN
MARK
BOOKS

Milwaukee, Wisconsin

This book is for educational purposes only
and does not replace medical or psychological treatment.

Published by
MavenMark Books,
a division of HenschelHAUS Publishing, Inc.
2625 S. Greeley St. Suite 201
Milwaukee, WI 53207
www.henschelHAUSbooks.com

Please contact the publisher for quantity discounts.

ISBN: 978-1-59598-178-3
Also available as a Kindle book, ISBN 978-1-59598-179-0

Library of Congress Cataloging Number: 2012936883

Printed in the United States of America.
Second printing.

For all who are searching…
May you find the peace within.

Table of Contents

Acknowledgments

I want to thank my husband, Dean, and my children, Jacob and Brandon, who make me feel healthy, wealthy, and happy every day.

I'd like to thank my entire family for their encouragement, love and support.

Thank you as well to my Inner Circle, a phenomenal group of women, my clients who make this work pure joy.

I thank the wonderful team who helped create this book: my editor Deanna Lohnes, my publisher Kira Henschel and her team at HenschelHAUS, Dachowski Photography, and all who have graced me with their assistance.

I thank God for all the blessings in my life.

Introduction

*H*ave you ever thought that your dreams were out of reach? Well, they aren't. They are not outside of you; they are within you. Keep reading because *Extreme Intuitive Makeover* will bring your dreams within reach. Are you ready? Of course you are—you were born for this!

Have you ever thought that there was more to life? There is. As human beings we use a small percentage of our brain. We are correct in thinking that there is something more and again, that something more is within us.

We have a left brain and a right brain. The left brain is logical, detail oriented, and facts rule here. It is practical and knows an object by name. The right brain is "big picture" oriented, uses symbols and images to decipher meaning, believes, appreciates, and is creative and intuitive. A large portion of the right hemisphere in our brain has been untapped. This hemisphere contains our connection to God, Spirit, and all that is. This is not a book about religion; it is sharing my experience and what has worked for me. I love the teachings of Jesus. I appreciate the wisdom of the Buddha and non-attachment and loving kindness.

This book is about helping you access the deep connection to God that is already within you. Within you there are riches beyond measure. Within you is the pearl beyond price. Within you is limitless creativity, abundance, peace, joy, and unconditional love. We need only to learn how to tap into this wondrous reserve. May this book bless you and bless all who will be served by you as you learn to access your intuition, purpose, inner well-being, health, wealth, and happiness.

Preface

*M*any people wonder what their purpose is in life. They wonder how they can achieve optimum health, wealth, and happiness. As an Intuitive Life Purpose Coach, I use my gift of intuition to help people access this information. I also teach ways to access intuition so that people can get this information for themselves. During a coaching session, it is not unusual for me to receive titles for books people are meant to write and business or workshop names for the heart-centered entrepreneur-to-be.

I named myself "The Intuitive Millionaire Coach" because I discovered the enormous wealth and riches within me. My body of work, all the life-changing information, books, art, oracle cards, self-help articles, and coaching came to me through my intuition. I felt as though I had discovered my inner intuitive millionaire. Now my passion, mission, and purpose include helping you find your inner intuitive millionaire.

As I work with clients, we go through what I call Wealth Centers. There are seven main spiritual centers in the body, known as chakras. These spiritual centers are our main connection to God. I use the word *intuition* to describe the information that comes through me from my Higher Self as connected to God, Spirit, Creator. There are keys to accessing your intuition, purpose, health, wealth and happiness. These keys are in your wealth centers, which are included in this book.

I am also including ideas to be creative in ways that you may not have thought about before. I am a self-taught, professional artist and published writer. In school, I was an average C student. I will show you how to create your own masterpieces and write, even if you think you can't. Even if you never thought of doing this before, you can.

Each Key contains an exercise to help you integrate the information. I will ask you to breathe consciously. When I refer to this, I would like you to breathe in deeply three times through your nose and out your mouth. This will help you connect to Spirit and move the energy in your body.

I am excited for your journey. Blessings and Love,

Anne

Key #1
Creativity

THE MONEY TREE OF LIFE –
CREATIVITY PAYS WELL

*G*reat sages and saints know about the great wealth within us, which includes the Kingdom of Heaven. Our next creative idea is not outside of us. If we take something we see as creative and use it for our own, that is considered copying. While people do this, it isn't as sustainable as your own unique and brilliant creations. God is the Creator.

We, as sparks of the Creator, have been given the full authority to connect to the Giant Genius of Spirit and create whatever we want in our lives. Creativity, by definition, encompasses new ideas, forms, and methods. Creativity is painting, drawing, writing, playing music, dancing, decorating. It is how we live our lives and how we make decisions for ourselves. We are the creators and designers of our lives. This is a powerful concept. Do you need to be a painter to be an artist? No—being artistic and creative is a way of life.

Being creative requires you to be aware of the present moment, to listen to your intuitive guidance in that moment and act on it. Being creative is not "thinking about it," but rather listening from within and doing from a place of spontaneity and knowingness. As you hear and act, you feel a powerful sense of trust. You will feel a sense of peace and joy as you create your life from moment to moment through listening to your intuition.

Painting is one vehicle of creative expression, one that has allowed me to tune into higher realms and unending inspiration. Writing is another avenue of creativity. I believe that there are many ways and that we are all creative. It is the way we approach life, with Faith, Hope and Love. After experiencing years of depression and anxiety, connecting with my creativity has helped me soar to new heights. I feel my inner strength and know that if I hit a wall, my creativity shows me new doors. I turn a corner and see new possibilities.

Why nurture our creativity? Well, when we don't, life can become dull and meaningless. We are all born with gifts and talents and our creativity allows us to express ourselves and share our gifts and talents with others. It frees us from isolation and helps us feel our sense of community. We can wake up joyful and inspired every day.

You experience wonder, miracles, freedom and peace beyond measure. You become inner directed, able to participate in the world with joy, independent of other's opinions. Despite what is happening in the outer world, you are connected through Spirit and live in an abundance of ideas and inspiration.

Creativity is a gift we are all born with. With surrender and trust with our Creator, we build a powerful bond. We can create unlimited possibilities as we co-create with the Universe. Our lives become enchanted and magical. Stop and listen to your loving inner guidance today and experience a joy filled life.

"The Kingdom of Heaven is Within." The first time that I heard or read those words, they helped me feel the light at the end of the tunnel. I no longer worry at all. Intuition, psychic awareness, psychic meaning of the Soul —all this inner work pertains to the inner world that many of us miss if we are too busy to notice, or too immersed in the earth plane world. Spiritual teachings encourage us to be *in* the world, but not *of* the world.

Many people have experienced power outages, earthquakes, and other major earth change experiences. It is more important than ever to learn to listen to your highest guidance that comes from within. We are so used to depending on outer resources for our well-being. In times of change, let us remember how divinely guided we are. Creativity is our connection with Spirit.

Before I felt creative, I felt depressed, like something was missing. Can you relate to this? Did you ever feel destined for creative genius? That book you dreamed about writing? The art you could show somewhere? Do you want to creatively design your life to match on the outside what you know to be true on the inside?

I felt this way and am here to tell you, that more and more, my reality has surpassed my dreams. When I was younger, my art teachers told me to forget about being an artist. I never dreamed of having my art sold, having commission work, and then displaying on the Laguna Beach Gallery Website.

We are here to experience abundance and to experience it to the fullest—and that's through our creativity!

EXERCISE TO GET THE CREATIVE JUICES FLOWING

Find a quiet spot and close your eyes. Breathe consciously and begin to imagine the color orange. See this sphere of orange energy grow brighter and brighter, feel its warmth.

Now begin to imagine what it would be like to feel like an artist in your life. Imagine that you are filled with ideas and inspirations beyond your wildest dreams. If you like to cook as a passion, imagine that award-winning dish on your own *Food Network Show*. If you want to teach others about what you have learned, see yourself in front of hundreds, thousands, or millions of people as they take notes on every word that comes out of your mouth. You are mesmerizing your audience and wowing them with your wisdom. They are cheering and clapping and smiling. If you have gone through life, you have learned something that you can teach, if you want to. You can teach a friend or millions of people. I believe it was Wealth Coach T. Harv Eker who said, "How you become a millionaire is by helping one person. If you can help one person, you can help a million."

Allow your will to be aligned with Divine Will and you have nothing to worry about. There is no such thing as dreaming too big.

Take out your journal and write down what you like to do for enjoyment such as gardening, cooking, or drawing. Did you ever think about painting or writing? Whatever it is you have thought about doing now is the time to write down those creative ideas. Later, we will formulate an action plan.

Key #2
Your Inner Creative Genius

UNLEASH IT

*H*ere are some ways to activate that inner creative genius of yours.

1. SET AN INTENTION

Intention is energy. We can hope and dream about being creative, but declaring by intention sets the wheels in motion with the Universe. The Universe wants to share the co-creation process with you. Say, "Thank you God, Spirit, that I am now receiving brilliant creative ideas and inspirations that fulfill my destiny and life's purpose."

2. PAY ATTENTION TO THOUGHTS AND FEELINGS

As a painter I am particularly attuned to color. As a writer, I love words. Begin to pay attention to what moves you. Have fun noticing what colors you are drawn to, what words interest you. Creativity in the arts can be writing, painting, drawing, music, and dance. Of course, creativity isn't limited to the arts; it can include cooking, decorating or sewing. Do not be intimidated by thinking that you need to be famous to fulfill your destiny in expressing yourself. Just do it. What moves you? Ask yourself this and let go of any judgments around the answers that you hear.

3. TAKE ACTION

Many know that they want to write. I say, buy a journal, meditate, and then write. I never took a painting class, but desperately wanted to paint. I bought the paints and painted. Classes are fine, but my message is that all that you need is within you. Act as if you already know what you are doing because you do know, deep within you, you know.

EXERCISE TO TAP INTO YOUR CREATIVITY

Find a quiet spot and close your eyes. Breathe consciously.

You are going to *Dream,* then *Do.* Imagine your finished product or new situation. Spend time feeling the feelings you wish to experience creatively. No matter what your dream is, begin to imagine it in your mind. Feel it as if it already is.

This is manifestation and co-creation with Spirit. It is Synergy, part your participation and part grace. Dream BIG! Go for it!

For example, I am creating a new website. I keep imagining it in my mind, I see the colors, and the design and fonts. I imagine my new book on the products page. This is creative visualization and it helps you create your life in the highest good.

You can also apply this technique with relationships. See yourself in harmony, balance, and love in your relationships. You can create the real thing by using your divinely focused vibration of energy. The Law of Attraction will magnetize your desires with your powerful thoughts.

Take out your journal and write about your ideas in terms of creative projects specifically. Try something new;

take a dance, art, or cooking class. As stated on the back of my first book, *Inner Visions: The Healing Path of Art*, "Art classes may be the best medicine for stress, anxiety, and can even help those with Parkinson's and terminal illness." The act of creativity generally makes people feel better. Expressing myself certainly played a role in my healing.

Key #3
Intuitive Painting

BREAKING ALL THE ART RULES

*W*hen you take an art class with me, prepare to experience something you have never experienced before. My art teachers might have a chuckle if they knew I was teaching art, and without a degree. The bold and brazen rebel is alive and well.

I did not excel in art class in school. It was usually pointed out to me that I was not as good as the person sitting next to me. I let that affect me for a decade or so until everything in my life changed. A boyfriend broke up with me, I started a new job, I was living in a new city, and knew no one. I was bored and desperate to become an artist because surely my old boyfriend might want me back if I was an artist! I figured I needed some paints and supplies to become this mysterious artist person.

I didn't take a class. I made it up as I went. It has worked out pretty well. I sell my work, I have been commissioned to paint a mural in a restaurant, and I hang my work in galleries. My favorite "ta-da" was when the Laguna Beach Gallery California website accepted my work. On a whim, I contacted them with a few JPEGs of my work.

What follows is everything I know about becoming an artist. You do not need to know how to draw or paint to take a course with me. I break all the art rules. My class is fun. I am including this here so that you can try it at home. You don't need an artist's studio — just a floor or a table.

I began my art career in my tiny apartment in 1992. Even if you thought you could never paint, you can. Try something new and creative because, remember, all art increases your intuition, which increases your well-being and ability to be abundant and joyful.

If you already paint, consider a new way of creating your masterpieces. I call it Intuitive Painting, because there is no thinking involved. You do not need to set up a still life or get a particular kind of paint. Here's how you do it:

EXERCISE TO PAINT WITH YOUR INTUITION

Go to your local crafts store. Grab a cart. Go to the paper section; pick out a pad of watercolor paper. Remember, no rules! I like Strathmore Watercolor cold press

11 x 15- inch size. Also choose a very large piece; my art store carries the 22 x 28-inch paper.

Next, find the paints. I paint with acrylic and watercolor paints. I bought those years ago and they work for me. Look at all the colors in both types of paints. Check prices, too; some are more costly than others. With your budget in mind, choose as many colors as you can. I like gold and silver metallic paints, too. It's good to have white. Other than that, I just get the colors I like and that's it. I always get glitter and would highly ecommend purchasing some glitter while you're at the craft store.

Now for brushes. Get a variety of sizes, no brand name or anything like that. I choose a big one to cover the big paper. I paint with big, medium, small, and fine-point brushes for detail, and sometimes a fan brush just to play. See how it goes.

When I started painting, I used paper plates to put my paints on and a paper cup to hold the water. Twenty years ago, I wasn't thinking about all those paper products and environmental issues; today, I use a ceramic mug to put water in and a reusable plastic palette.

To protect my rug or table from paint, I get shower curtains from the Dollar Store. You can do whatever feels right. Have a roll of paper towels nearby to use in a technique I will talk about shortly.

Now you need to set up your art space. I wear an old t-shirt and leggings that already have paint on them. I cover my rug. When I lived in an apartment, I used a towel on the floor. Now I have my large shower curtain. If you have bad knees or can't work on the floor, cover a table.

I get out my CDs and choose some ahead of time. I blast music the whole time I am painting. My CD player has to have a replay button because I will get in the zone with a song and will repeat it over and over. Do what feels good to you.

Get your mug of water and your paper, big or small. In my art classes, we use both sizes of paper. Each offers a different experience. Have your brushes near your water and near your paper.

Now for the fun part. Take your tubes of paint and squeeze out the colors one by one, just any way. You can use the palette or the paper, or whatever feels right. Watercolor and acrylic, no rhyme or reason is fine. Have your music playing. Sit down with your paper in front of you and pick up your brush. Dip it in water. Dip it in paint. Now *paint*! If you chose the big paper, it's good to use the big brush to cover the surface first.

Here's how I paint intuitively. I just pick whatever color I like and apply it, any which way. I just keep choosing paint. I paint over colors. Just paint, rather than trying to create an image. I call this "building up the background." I use lots of water and lots of paint. Sometimes I take a paper towel and smooth out the whole thing, almost erasing everything I've done. I have nothing in mind. I just paint with abandon, surrounded by the loud music I love. I can do this for hours. Then an idea will come to me, a star or flower or anything. I take a smaller finer brush and draw the star with a new color right over my layered background.

I have been known to paint a near-perfect image then "erase" it by dumping water on it and moving my paper towel over it. One of my students gasped when I told her to do this. I just knew she had more in her; what she thought was her painting wasn't. She didn't like the idea, but she took my suggestion, poured water all over the flower she had painted, and started over. I will never forget her finished painting. It was an undersea view of a treasure chest, very mermaid-dolphin-wonderful. She cried tears of joy that I pushed her past her limits. She framed it and people even came to her home, asking to buy it.

I let go of outcome while I paint. I just know when to stop and when to keep going. As an example, I build up a background, get a small brush, paint a star, and then throw various colors of glitter all over it. I also like to draws spirals and sometimes use the back of my brush to draw with. I have squeezed paint right from the tube onto the paper. One time, I swirled the tube around as I squeezed the paint out and it looked like an eye. I have it framed in my living room.

You can call on your Higher Self, Angels, Masters of Light, or the Fairies to paint with you. You can just put color on paper, add water, and swirl your brush around. Watercolor is great for that. There is magic in intuitive painting. Try it for yourself!

Key #4
Intuitive Journaling

JOURNAL YOUR ANSWERS

There are methods I have heard about to gain information for yourself from writing. One of these methods is called automatic writing. The problem is that we have egos and information coming to us in automatic writing is not always quality information. As a person who uses her intuition as a profession, it is very important that I receive the best guidance for my clients. Say an intention prayer and channel your Higher Self in writing. In another key, we will talk about Higher Self channeling as spoken out loud.

EXERCISE TO FIND THE ANSWERS THROUGH WRITING

Find a quiet spot and close your eyes. Breathe consciously. Call on your Higher Self. Thank God you are in a protected space. Call in the Masters of Light. Call on the Angels. Ask for your highest and best, better than you could ever imagine. Thank God you are a pure and clear channel today.

Now ask your question. Take out your journal and write and write without taking your pen off the page. Start with Dearest (your name), then allow the information to come through you without editing. You may have to write through any ego coming in, but keep writing page after page without thinking at all. Don't get your mind involved. Don't edit yourself in any way. Keep writing until you can write no more. Go back and read what you wrote and feel the resonance of your own wise words.

Key #5
Intuitive Writing

HELPING YOURSELF SAVES THE WORLD

*I*n my wildest high school dreams, did I see myself as a published author? Maybe for a split second, followed by the voice that said "Are you kidding? You can't write." I never got much above a C in English. It did not look like I would be awarded any merits of honor for my writing any time soon, much less have published works. What would I say and who would read it?

Publishing a book was indeed a turning point in my life. It proved to me that if I could do it, anyone could, if he or she wanted to. You see, we have all gone through life and learned some things—some things other people may not have learned, or some things people may not need to learn, but would enjoy reading about. Maybe you know someone who can benefit from your school of hard knocks.

I have been published in many article directories. My self-help articles have gone viral and been published on many websites. I also have been published in several magazines including *Aspire Magazine* and *Martha's Vineyard Island Inspiration Magazine*. It was nice to have my article featured on the cover, right next to Dr. Deepak Chopra's.

Many of you are writers at heart, whether you have written anything or not. You have a dream to write. I can see why! It is glorious. In my coaching programs, I often support aspiring writers. The results have been very rewarding, particularly when they actually get published. Then they have the reward of knowing they have helped someone, because they took the time to write about their experience. For many people, writing is an ideal creative exercise. It keeps us spiritually fit when we express ourselves from the heart.

EXERCISE TO TURN YOUR LIFE EXPERIENCE INTO HELPING OTHERS — WRITE A SELF-HELP ARTICLE AND PUBLISH IT

Find a quiet spot and get out your notebook or computer. Begin to think about something that you are passionate about. Here are some questions that will get you thinking about writing or why you haven't written yet. These questions will assist in breaking any blocks that you may have around writing.

- Have you ever thought about writing? If yes, imagine what those thoughts were and write them down.

- How did you do in high school English class?

- Imagine writing your book. Is it fiction or non-fiction? Describe it now.

- Did you receive the message as a child that children were seen and not heard? Did you feel inferior in communicating and expressing your feelings?

- What do you know how to do?

- What is important to you? What are you passionate about?

- Ask your Higher Self and write down four titles or topics you could write about.

As you went through the questions, could you begin to see areas around communication that have held you stuck in any way? If you are willing, ask that Spirit clear away any doubt or fears you have had around writing.

The first article I ever wrote and published was *Six Ways to Access Your Intuition*. After realizing my intuition was so helpful, I knew I could write about my process. I had experienced some unkindness in my life, then I decided to write an article called *Kindness Matters*. I wrote about what I felt passionate about.

Since then, I have written many articles. One way to write is straightforward—just write about what matters to you. Another way of writing articles is by using what I call "the formula." You take a topic, write a short paragraph about it, then list one, two, three, four, or more ideas that support your topic. Write several sentences about each supporting idea. Close with a short paragraph to sum it up.

At the end of the book, you will find sample articles I have written and published. You can see which one is straightforward writing and which one uses "the formula." All the articles have my bio at the end. In a later Key, we will work on your bio. You will need one at the end of every article that you submit so that people can find you and help you build your brand.

Blessings for writing from your heart as you inspire others with all that you have learned in wisdom!

ARTICLE DIRECTORIES I HAVE SUBMITTED ARTICLES TO:
www.ezinearticles.com
www.articledashboard.com
www.goarticles.com

When you go on these sites, click on "Submit Articles" and follow the directions. It is really quite easy.

I love writing, for it creates infinite possibilities in your life and establishes you as an expert in your field. What you came here to do in terms of your Soul's purpose can be wonderfully expressed through writing about what you care about. I am now published in magazines and you can be, too. I use my articles as a foundation for seminars and speeches as well.

There is a lot you can do with just one article. In addition to using the information in workshops, you can add it to your website, and more. You can create a blog and post it there. I recommend using www.wordpress.com to create your own blog and post your articles. It is very easy to set up your own blog and begin to express yourself. Post your blog link on Facebook or Twitter. Get your message out into the world.

Key #6
You Are Wealthy

UNDERSTANDING YOUR WEALTH CENTERS

*T*hroughout the ages great sages and saints have delivered the Divine message that the Kingdom of Heaven is within us. This is not just a nice idea, but a measurable metaphysical reality I have discovered through intuitively coaching people.

There are seven Wealth Centers that contain great information about how wealthy from within you really are. The Wealth Centers are spiritual centers related to the Chakra system. It is possible to clear these centers of anything in your life that has caused you to be less than joyful. Your Wealth Centers are your spiritual connections to God, to your Higher Self, to your spiritual gifts in your physical body. They contain everything that has ever happened to you, including what your fifth grade teacher said that is still affecting you today.

In my Intuitive Millionaire Program, I developed the Wealth Center system based on the Chakra system. I call them Wealth Centers to demonstrate that inner riches, gifts, talents, and strengths are within us. We can access them with some tools, tips, and techniques that I will share with you in this book.

We will now go through each Wealth Center to help you gain a deeper appreciation and understanding of the riches within you, which include your intuition and life's purpose. Before we begin the journey through our Wealth Centers, here is an exercise to help you prepare to meet the "Great You Within."

EXERCISE TO CONNECT YOU WITH THE WEALTH WITHIN

Take a moment to find a quiet space where you can connect with your inner being. Breathe consciously as described in the introduction.

Call on your highest Divine Self. Call on your highest Teachers and Guides; call on the Masters of Light, on Spirit. Imagine for a moment that you are at peace. Know that everything is OK and that you are safe. Begin to imagine from the base of your spine a glowing red energy. This is your Foundation Wealth Center. Thank it for its safety, its security, and connection to purpose and Mother Earth.

In your mind's eye, move up to just below your belly button. Imagine a vibrant glowing orange energy. This is your Creativity and Truth Wealth Center. Thank it for its feelings, its creativity, its sensuality, sexuality, vibrancy, aliveness, and for knowing your True Self.

Moving up to your stomach area, your solar plexus, see a glowing yellow energy as bright as the sun. This is your Power Wealth Center. Thank it for its alignment with Divine Will, for its inner power, its power, courage, and freedom from the opinions of others.

Moving up to the heart area, see a glowing green healing energy. This is your Love Wealth Center. Thank it for its unconditional love, giving and receiving unconditional love to yourself and others, for its Divine portal, for being the gateway to Divine wisdom and consciousness.

Now imagine a light blue glowing energy at your throat center. This is your Communication Wealth Center. Thank it for its healthy, balanced communication, for its ability to express itself from the heart with authenticity and honesty creating no harm.

Now see a glowing bluish-purple energy between your eye brows. This is your Intuition Wealth Center.

Thank it for its spiritual gifts, psychic abilities, clairvoyance, ability to translate information from the Higher Realms of Spirit and the Angels, Ascended Master Teachers, and Masters of Light.

Moving to the top of your head, see a beautiful violet light glowing with energy, this is your Source Wealth Center. Thank it for its connection to Spirit, to the Christ Consciousness, for the connection to Light that holds all the information you need to live your highest good and best life.

Now that you are connected to the Divine Power within, let's go through each wealth center one at a time to further heal, clear, and activate the wealth and inner power within you.

Key #7
The Foundation Wealth Center

Don't Build Your House Upon Sand

At the very base of your spine is the Foundation Wealth Center. Many experiences we have had since an early age are contained in this center. Working with clients includes removing the false beliefs that are held there. When we believe the things that people have told us in this center, it is as though we have built our house upon sand.

Foundation Wealth Center issues include feeling safe, secure, that you have a roof over your head, food to eat, and that your basic needs are met. You feel grounded and solid in your body. You feel connected to your purpose. What can happen starting in childhood is that we absorb or take on other people's beliefs. We are especially vulnerable to the beliefs of those in authority. If we don't heal those beliefs, we live as though the other shoe is about to drop, feeling unstable, living in a state of fear, and not really knowing why.

Sometimes, when we are young, we may get a message that we can't afford things or that we are inadequate and we take that belief on. We live that out in our lives. These are messages that can create a shakiness to this center at your core.

I recommend going back over your life and allowing feelings you may have stifled to come forth. Begin to recognize where those messages came from. Start to see that whoever the people were who attempted to plant those seeds were feeling fear or pain themselves. Have compassion for them, and see the messages as separate from your Truth. No longer identify with the false beliefs. Understand, forgive, and see that many people have attempted to avoid pain by projecting it onto someone else. Forgive yourself for taking that pain into your experience.

Our truth is that we are divinely guided by Spirit, by Guides, by Angels in every moment. No matter what has happened to you in the past, it is never too late to create a solid foundation for yourself on which to move forward.

One way to enhance the feeling of groundedness is being in nature. Surround yourself in nature where you can clearly feel and see the support of Mother Earth. Notice the cycles of nature around you. Leaves may fall off the trees, but they come back in the spring. Notice the herbs, flowers, the bounty and abundance around you. Walk in nature; notice the trees and the strong, wise energy they emit. Spending time in nature is very helpful for our Foundation Wealth Center. There are healing properties in nature that can affect us positively in our emotional, physical, and spiritual bodies.

EXERCISE FOR A STRONG FOUNDATION WEALTH CENTER

Get yourself a journal and a pen. Imagine or find a spot in nature where you feel serene. Breathe consciously. Begin to connect with the energy at the base of your spine. Imagine a glowing red sphere of energy. Call on your Higher Divine Self to support you. Ask for clearing and healing of any messages you may have received in the past that have thwarted your feeling of safety and security in the world. Gently feel the energy move and release in this center.

Now begin to focus your energy and will in this center and proclaim, "I am safe, I am nurtured, I am loved."

Allow ideas or thoughts to come to you about taking action in any area where you felt stuck. Write in your journal any ideas that come to you around taking action in your life, like calls you need to make or anything you may have been putting off. The very act of writing your ideas from this exercise will help you feel strong, capable and grounded in this center. Feel yourself filled with unconditional love for yourself and others in this center. Take action on what you wrote. You are the strong Foundation for your life. Feel unconditional love for yourself and others in this center.

Key #8
The Creativity and Truth Wealth Center

FIND YOUR BLISS

Your Creativity and Truth Wealth Center is located just above the Foundation Wealth Center and just below your solar plexus/stomach area. This center has to do with your creativity, sensuality, sexuality, and honoring your feelings, vibrancy and joy. Sometimes in our lives, we are given messages by other people that include the message we are not creative. We hear that we have no right to feel the way we do, that life is a chore, that play is for children.

The truth is that these are not accurate messages; they are false beliefs. The truth of who we are is that we are creative. We are sparks from our Creator. We have unique gifts and talents. We have a right to our feelings. It is our birthright to experience joy.

When we suppress our feelings and emotions and live each day just getting by, we can begin to experience depression in this energy center. It is healthy to honor ourselves and our feelings. It is helpful to channel our emotions in a healthy, balanced, and creative way.

One way to honor this wealth center is by *knowing* you are creative. Creativity can include painting, drawing, dancing, writing, cooking, decorating, or finding creative solutions in your life. There is no limit to ways you can be creative.

EXERCISE TO HELP YOU CLEAR AND ACTIVATE YOUR CREATIVITY AND TRUTH WEALTH CENTER

Have your journal and pen ready. Find a quiet spot and close your eyes. Breathe consciously.

Now begin to focus on the area just below your stomach. Imagine a glowing orange sphere of energy. Begin to go back in time to an age where you remember what it felt like to play. Sense the feeling of joy as you know there is nothing you have to do and nowhere you have to be. Feel that feeling and know that you can bring it into the now.

Here in present time, feel the feeling of joyful play. Imagine that you are finger painting, feeling the spontaneity, painting without rules and outside the lines. You are free and joyful.

In this feeling, ask your Higher Self "How can I continue this feeling every moment of my life? I am joyful, I am free, and I receive creative ideas. I know that the truth of my being is joy. Show me how to honor my feelings. Thank you for showing me ways to be more creative in my life."

Now take out your journal and write down what comes to you. Enjoy the freedom and play for its own sake, just because you are enough. Feel unconditional love for yourself and others in this center. Thank your Higher Self for helping you uncover your joy.

Key #9
The $Power$ $Wealth$ $Center$

YOU ARE INDOMITABLE

*A*t your solar plexus, the area of your stomach where you feel your gut feelings, is your Power Wealth Center. This center has to do with feeling your will aligned with Divine Will. You feel your inner power and you are not at the mercy of the opinions of other people. You cannot be bullied or feel helpless, weak, or powerless when this center is activated. You are indomitable.

Many of us have suffered greatly in this Wealth Center. We may have been taught that other people's feelings and opinions mattered more than ours. We may have been taught to manipulate others in order to experience a feeling of power or control in our lives. We may have experienced what it feels like to be manipulated or controlled by other people.

The truth is, we have our own power and we do not need it from other people. We do not need to give our power away. The true source of our power comes from within. We are all connected to the Creator of the Universe. Now that is real and lasting power.

Some of us have been taught to fear our own power. True power is kind; true power is gentle and strong. True power cannot put down. Love is the most powerful force in the Universe. Love can heal all wounds. Love is real power and there is nothing to fear about using that kind of power.

Know that you are strong within yourself, that you have Divine Power within you. You don't have to sacrifice yourself to other people so that you can look good and "be nice." This is counter-productive. True power resonates with the Law of Attraction. Anything you do to "people please" at the expense of yourself is a low vibration and will not attract into your life your highest good.

It takes courage to say "No" when that is the best thing for you to do. It takes courage to be yourself and not to worry about what people think of you.

Know this: you are a beacon of light. Although it may be challenging to live your life on your terms, authentic and honest, you are doing more good by being yourself than you could ever imagine. You will resonate with truth, honesty, authenticity, and real power. When you do this, you set an example for other people to do the same, should they choose to. When you dim your true power, it serves no one.

EXERCISE TO TAP INTO YOUR
DIVINE, POWER WEALTH CENTER

Have your journal ready. Find a quiet spot and close your eyes. Breathe consciously.

Imagine a glowing bright yellow sphere of energy, as bright as the sun, right at your stomach area. Feel your power within you. Ask your Higher Self to align your will with Divine Will. Begin to relax as you move deeper and deeper into the comfort of knowing you are aligned with Divine Will. Feel the deep trust that comes with this connection. Imagine your life in every area aligned with this power. See your relationships with others as harmonious, for you are connected to the true source of power within you.

Feel free from the opinions of other people. Feel the power to make decisions for your life based on your own highest good. Feel the abundance and prosperity that comes with this inner power. You are aligned with the greatest power in the Universe. You are creating your life from this connection.

Write down anything that comes to you around your alignment with Divine Will. What are you doing for work, how are your personal relationships, love relationships, friendships, have they changed now that you are in your power? How does that look?

Feel unconditional love for yourself and others in this center.

Key #10
The Love Wealth Center

TRUE LOVE HEALS ALL WOUNDS

When it comes to the heart, we can experience elation or heartbreak or anything in between. Our heart is our feeling center and the place of our deepest knowing. Matters of the heart can include giving and receiving love and loving others unconditionally.

When we are out of balance in the Love Wealth Center, we can experience emotional pain. We give and give out of obligation, desperation, and the need for approval or receiving something in return. We can take and take from others and not give anything back. These are some examples of an imbalance in this energy center.

The heart is meant to love unconditionally. This is one of the last lessons on earth and often the most difficult to achieve. We will experience heartbreak and loss over and over until we realize in our Souls that nothing real is ever threatened. True love lasts and everything we offer in true, selfless love and service is rewarded in its own way. That's not why we do it. Unconditional love requires a love for oneself. Loving ourselves is not selfish, despite what many of us were taught to believe. Knowing deep in our Souls that we are children of God and are worthy just because we are alive can help us transform feelings of self-loathing into feelings of pure love and forgiveness for ourselves and others.

Many of us are not aware of the seeds of self-hatred that have dominated our lives. Over and over, we tend to beat ourselves up for not being "perfect," for saying or doing the "wrong" thing. We are here to learn soul lessons and realize that we were never separate from God. We are made in the image of our Creator.

When we awaken to this understanding, we begin to see the inherent goodness, gifts, talents, and connection to God and the Higher Realms of Beings that are always near to us.

When you connect with your heart center, you are able to access the portal of Divine wisdom. You have access to cosmic consciousness and the very mind of God through your heart. The Bible passage "Ask and it is given, Knock and it shall be opened to you" refers to the idea that anything asked for shall be granted with the highest good through love. What a gift it is that we can experience Heaven on Earth, now, through our Heart.

EXERCISE TO AWAKEN AND ACTIVATE
YOUR LOVE WEALTH CENTER

Find a quiet spot, close your eyes, and breathe consciously.

Begin to focus on your heart center. See a brilliant, glowing, green sphere of energy in this area. Call upon your Higher Self and ask to be shown where you are experiencing pain, loss, or lack of forgiveness. Imagine a blanket of comfort and pure love surrounding you as you do this exercise, gently reminding you that you are never alone.

Acknowledge the feelings that come up and honor each and every one. When you are ready, ask to release any pain or emotional suffering and give it to the angels surrounding you now. Breathe deeply as you release these emotions.

Now ask to be given Divine understanding. This Divine wisdom will serve you moving forward. You are now able to receive from the heart of our Creator the deep understanding of every situation in your life. You are now seeing all through the eyes of Love.

Write in your journal anything that comes to you as new information on anything that has troubled you in the past. See yourself filled with unconditional love for yourself and others in your Heart.

Key #11
The Communication Wealth Center

THE POWER OF THE WORD

*A*t your throat area is the Communication Wealth Center. This energy center involves our verbal and written communication. It is the center of Divine expression. If this area is not balanced, we may find ourselves stifling our emotions and words, or we may experience the extreme imbalance in communication as we yell and scream to be heard.

We may have received messages growing up that we were not important and that what we had to say was not important. Many of us have been crippled and paralyzed in our expression. All feelings eventually come to the surface, which is why it is so important to clear and energize this Communication center with a positive flow of energy. Remember that any communication made from the heart never causes harm.

What often happens in our communication is that we skip the heart and speak from a place of pain or defensiveness. Balanced, authentic communication is an art we can master. It requires that we stand in our truth and accept responsibility for ourselves and our feelings. When we are in touch with our true power from our Power Wealth Center and our Love from our Love Wealth Center, it does not matter what other people think of us while we are communicating. Their resistance is theirs and we do not try to change them. We are communicating out of deep respect, while honoring who we are and who they are.

I often tell my clients when working with them intuitively that it is not just me and them having a conversation; it's me, my Higher Self and guides, and their Higher Self and guides. I speak to their greatness. I speak to the highest aspect of them. This creates a communication based on the truth of who they are, not their limitations or perceived wounds and hurts. The truth is that we are all great beings having an experience on Earth to remember who we are. When we communicate with each other while keeping this in mind, it is easy to respect and honor each other while maintaining harmony and peace in our communications.

EXERCISE FOR CLEARING AND ACTIVATING YOUR
COMMUNICATION WEALTH CENTER

Find a quiet spot and close your eyes. Breathe consciously. Imagine a light blue sphere of energy in your throat area. As you do this, call on your Higher Self and ask for the clearing of any unbalanced communication in this area.

Feel yourself now unstuck in your communication. See yourself speaking your truth authentically from your heart to the person who has not listened to you in the past or present time. Honor yourself for speaking up now from your heart, while honoring the person that you are imagining speaking with. Say how you feel, forgive them and yourself for any miscommunication.

Now ask to be cleared from any anger, hostility or repressed emotions that would lead to the unbalanced communication of yelling and screaming. See yourself calmly being heard and acknowledged. Know that moving forward, you are free to communicate your feelings, knowledge, along with your creative gifts and talents, from a place of Divine love for yourself and others.

Pick up your journal and write down anything that comes to you around expressing yourself from your Higher Self now. Feel unconditional love for yourself and others in your Communication Wealth Center.

Key #12
The Intuition Wealth Center

YOU HAVE SPIRITUAL GIFTS

Your Intuition Wealth Center is located between your eyebrows, in the center of your forehead. This spot is often referred to as your Third Eye. Know and understand that we are all born with spiritual gifts, such as clairvoyance (clear seeing), clairsentience (clear feeling), claircognizance (clear knowing), and clairaudience (clear hearing). These gifts from God are our birthright.

Many of us have shut down these gifts with the misunderstanding that they could create harm for ourselves and others. It is the time now in our history to reclaim what is ours, which is to be used in the highest good. When we understand from an intuitive perspective what is happening in any given moment, we have the power to make the wisest choices for ourselves.

Our spiritual gifts offer us insights into the higher truth of any given situation. We can receive information from God, the Angels, the Masters of Light, and our Higher Selves. This is information that cannot be read in a book or logically explained. When we are connected to our intuition, we are connected to the highest Divine wisdom in the Universe. We have the ability to tune into any information on the cosmic highway.

Not all of this information is in the highest good and there are psychics who do tune into fear and doubt. I teach a prayer that allows me to tune into the highest realms for information for myself.

Receiving this information is life-changing. You don't know how you know, you just do. When you receive clear information from your intuition, the part of you connected to God, you will make the best decisions for your life and experience much more ease, grace, and flow in your life.

EXERCISE TO CLEAR AND ACTIVATE
YOUR INTUITION WEALTH CENTER

Find a quiet spot and close your eyes. Breathe consciously. Imagine a glowing indigo-colored sphere of energy between your brows. Feel the pulsing energy gently open your third eye of intuition and activate your spiritual gifts.

As you feel the light energy gently open this center, you may feel a tingling or warmth there. Now ask your Higher Self to remove any blocks you may have in this area of intuition.

Affirm that now you are open to receiving the highest good and most clear information based on the highest truths now. Affirm that you are open to enlightenment in all areas of your life. Affirm that you receive clear knowing, clear seeing, clear hearing and clear feelings regarding your life.

Thank the Holy Spirit for speaking to you in every moment as you are always guided and never alone. Pick up your journal and write down anything that comes to you around your spiritual gifts and how you will use them in service to yourself and others.

Fill the area of your Intuition Wealth Center with unconditional love for yourself and others.

Key #13
The Source Wealth Center

YOU ARE NEVER ALONE

*L*ocated at the top of your head is your Source Wealth Center. You are connected to God, Creator. You always have been and you always will be. The promise of God is that we are not left as orphans. We have free will and can choose to experience any kind of separation or illusion of that if we choose to. With a deep love and respect for us, God gave us free will.

If we choose to align our will with Divine will, we will feel an invincible connection to God in our being. Nourishing this connection will bring about much comfort and grace in our lives. Acknowledging this connection will allow us to feel expanded and infinite. This is because we have a Divine potential, a blueprint, that we are born with that can help us realize the Self in infinite ways.

One way to nourish this connection to Source is to put our awareness there. Our thoughts, will, and intention have great power. We can also take the time to still our thoughts and quietly meditate, that is, to be quiet and mindful of hearing the voice of God within us. This voice is loving, knowing, peaceful, and infinitely wise. We know this voice. On the other hand, the voice of ego creates fear, doubt, lack, and worry.

When you hear the voice of ego, gently guide yourself back to the still voice within your Soul that tells you everything is OK. From that place, you can ask questions and receive clear guidance for your life. If you are in fear, anger or upset, you will not be able to hear the Higher Self and its infinite wisdom. Your Higher Divine Self is always connected to God and you have the potential for hearing its guidance 24/7.

EXERCISE FOR CLEARING AND ACTIVATING YOUR SOURCE WEALTH CENTER

Find a quiet spot and close your eyes. Breathe consciously and imagine a glowing sphere of violet-white light at the top of your head. Feel a white light energy expand up to the heavens as a column of white light.

Now imagine that light coming back down through the top of your head, your crown chakra, as white-gold Christed light. The light enters the top of your head, moves down through all of your energy centers, and out through the bottom of your feet deep into the core of Mother Earth. Feel any unstable or discordant energy within you go out with that light into the Earth to be transmuted and transformed. Feel the energy of grounded, stable white-gold Christed light return up through your energy centers and feel your heart expand with it.

Your connection to God is intact, cleared, and activated. You are able to move through the world as a being of Light, with a clear knowing of your purpose and mission.

Take out your journal and write down any thoughts that come to you around your purpose and how you are here to create from your highest Divine potential. Ask to be shown hidden gifts and talents that have been dormant and are now ready to be awakened and celebrated. Write without stopping for five full minutes. Feel unconditional love for yourself and others in your Crown Source Wealth Center.

Key #14
Meditation

OPENING THE DIVINE PORTAL

*Y*ears ago, I suffered from debilitating depression and anxiety. They paralyzed me, culminating in what I now call a "very dark night of the soul." I was unable to sleep, eat, or function for a period of time. At my local health food store I picked up a spiritual magazine that had an article titled "Receiving the Divine." I knew instinctively that it would help me.

I ordered the recommended book and DVD on Kriya Yoga meditation by Norman Paulsen as he had received it from Ascended Master Yogananda and began to practice it. Now, I had heard of meditation over the years, but was never quite able to do it. This type of yoga is not just a meditation; it is a spiritual tool to open Divine consciousness.

I practiced this meditation technique as described and soon broke through the paralyzing depression that had had its grip on me. I felt the flood of creativity and light come through me so strongly that I began to write my first book.

I had never considered myself to be a writer. I never received good grades in English in school, and yet, after practicing this meditation, I felt information flowing through me so strongly that I picked up pen and paper and began to write.

I had opened the Divine flow of light, energy, and information that was meant to come through me after practicing this meditation. I heard in my intuition, "You will write a book," and I saw in my mind's eye the book itself. My channels to Divine guidance were now open and my life was forever changed. After I wrote my book, *Inner Visions – The Healing Path of Art*, I contacted Norman Paulsen and he flew me to California, and actually published my book. I was now a Kriya Yoga Initiate, in the lineage of the great Masters.

Since then, I have learned that miracles can and do happen. From that experience, my life has opened more and more to my life's purpose and my connection to the greatest source of inspiration and creativity within me continues to flow abundantly. I could not write the book you are holding now without talking about Kriya Yoga meditation.

EXERCISE FOR REALIZING YOUR TRUE SELF
AND CONNECTION TO GOD

Please visit www.sunburstonline.org and explore.

Key #15
Gratitude

EVERYTHING IS VIBRATION

Several years ago, on her popular television program, Oprah Winfrey discussed keeping a gratitude journal. Gratitude is a portal, a gateway, to receiving wisdom. When you express gratitude to the Universe, it sends back to you more and more. You are giving gratitude and as you give, you are creating a space within to receive. It is helpful to remember, as often as possible, what you are grateful for.

Seeing the glass half-full and not half-empty is powerful. When you are grateful, the Universe gives back to you. When you are grateful, you feel joy. Joy is a magnet and more and more opportunities and reasons to be grateful will appear in your life.

Everything is vibration. Fear and doubt are vibrations, love and gratitude are vibrations. On a vibrational scale, fear and doubt are lower vibrations; love and gratitude are higher vibrations.

In the world, like energy seeks like energy. Thus, if you are radiating lower energy vibrations, you attract that energy into your life. The good news is that you do have some control over this. With this understanding of how energy and vibration works, you can begin to think and feel thoughts with a higher vibration, such as love, joy, gratitude, and appreciation. What you put your focus on expands. In a higher state of well-being, you will be able to hear your intuition more clearly.

EXERCISE FOR ATTRACTING HIGHER VIBRATIONS AND HIGHEST GOOD EXPERIENCES INTO YOUR LIFE

Find a quiet spot and close your eyes. Breathe consciously until you feel any heavy or dense energies leave you. Imagine with each in breath, that you are breathing in love and gratitude. With each out breath, breathe out fear, doubt, or worry.

In this relaxed space, breathing comfortably, begin to imagine the most beautiful blue sky above you. Feel the rays of the sun warm you. Begin to notice the trees, flowers, and land that surround you. Feel the abundance and supply that is neverending. Let any feeling of lack leave you.

Imagine everything that is in your highest good appears now and you experience profound joy. Feel gratitude for all the gifts you are receiving and smile. More of these experiences are on the way every time you practice this exercise.

See and feel yourself receiving all the well-being, all the gifts in your highest good. Accept these gifts and feel your heart swell with gratitude.

Now take out your journal and write down five things that you are grateful for now. May you be blessed with gratitude.

Key #16
Intention

ASK AND IT IS GIVEN

The door to inner guidance swings wide open as we set our intention. Heavenly help is always available. Because we have free will, our angels and guides are waiting for us to ask. As we ask, we receive answers. True inner guidance responds in a kind and gentle voice. Energy flows where will and intention are directed. This makes us powerful co-creators with Spirit.

Everything intended with the will of the Divine Will will be made manifest. It is only our lack of this awareness that prevents or slows down our Divine manifestations. Many of us were led to believe that we had no power, that things just happened. When we take the reins, drive the cars of our lives with the intention of aligning with the Will of God, we are creating a powerful energy of intention that will be supported fully.

When we choose *not* to use the power of intention, we will feel a lack of power in our lives. We feel as though things are happening around us or to us. By using our power of intention, we can create our lives and manifest or bring into our realities wonderful and magnificent creations and experiences.

EXERCISE TO EFFECTIVELY ENGAGE OUR POWER TO INTEND THE HIGHEST GOOD IN OUR LIVES

Find a quiet spot and close your eyes. Breathe consciously as you begin to connect with the will within you that is invincible. You have the power to align your will with Divine Will, whereby fully activating the forces of Heaven to intervene on your behalf.

Affirm out loud "My will is aligned with Your Will, God." Begin to feel the inner strength within you as you intend that your highest good now be manifest on earth.

"Thank you God. I now manifest my highest good as I intend that all areas of my life be supported in the highest good. With the full authority, as a child of God, as in accordance with Divine Will and Law, all of my dreams in accordance with this Will are now fully realized and made manifest. Thank you for answering my prayers and intentions."

Take out your journal and write down your powerful intentions as aligned with the Divine Will for your life.

And so it is.

Key #17
Downtime

ALLOW AND RECEIVE

fter setting our intention and meditating, it is beneficial to remain open and in a state of allowing. When we are busiest, we rarely hear our intuition. Remember that quiet and stillness are highly conducive to hearing our guidance. Creative ideas can flow in stillness.

There are masculine and feminine energies in the Universe. Masculine energies provide information in any given moment. The masculine energies in the Universe are giving us information, inspiration, and creative ideas. We must be still enough in our being to stop and create the space to receive this information. The feminine energies are receptive. It is important to have balanced energies within us, that is, the energies of giving and receiving.

To balance my energies, I find it helpful to turn off the TV, phone, or any other distractions that prevent me from clearly hearing and receiving this information. I am reminded of a plane in the air, circling the runway, looking for a place to land. We are the receptors, the receivers of information, as channeled from the Light, God, Creator, Source.

Included in our Divine potential for making manifest on Earth our dreams and visions, as aligned with the highest good, is the ability to receive creative inspirations. These creative inspirations can change our life for the better. What I call *downtime* is the time we take to be still and intend that we connect with our Divine Source to receive the creative ideas and inspiration.

Taking action on those ideas will follow, but for now let us create the space to receive.

Exercise to Allow and Receive Divine Ideas and Inspirations

Take a moment to be still, find a quiet space, close your eyes and breathe consciously as you focus your attention on the quiet and stillness within you.

Ask your Higher Self to be present and ask that anything blocking your reception to your highest good be removed. Feel the sense of receiving abundant ideas and inspirations. Feel dormant, creative ideas begin to rise up and inform and enlighten you. Allow your mind and heart to open to all creative ideas as given from God to you, in the highest good, now.

Take out your journal and begin to write down any ideas or inspirations that come to you. Do not try to figure out *how* to do what you are receiving, just receive the ideas and allow the joy that comes from knowing that your greatest good is manifesting now.

Key #18
Worthiness

AN ENERGY THAT INVOKES GRACE

It is important to remember that we are children of God. Expecting the best when we ask for clarity and answers is helpful. There are ego voices that tell us we are not worthy. Be aware that messages from the ego are not our true reality. We are sparks from our Creator. When we approach God with worthiness, he responds powerfully.

Worthiness is another high vibration energy that invokes the Grace of God. It is an energy of inherent trust and faith. Jesus told us to be like little children. This does not mean being childish, but rather childlike, innocent in the purity of trust and faith that we will be provided for and receive the blessings in store for us.

I often think of Christmastime and receiving gifts from Santa. I see a benevolent God, similar to my parents, wanting to give my brother and me wonderful gifts. It is a love I receive from Divine Spirit that does not have to be earned.

I once painted a painting called *Spiritual World*. In it, faces of Ascended Masters showed up as faces from the Divine. That experience showed me to expect miracles.

With this healthy and enthusiastic space of joy and expectancy, I raise the vibrational energy in my being to match the benevolent energy of God. From that place, I become an open receiver and channel of the highest good.

Everyday miracles can and do occur. From a place of high vibrational energy, I ask for my highest good and I receive it. I ask to be shown my purpose in life. I hear my intuition clearly as I am now on the wavelength and frequency of the highest realms.

EXERCISE TO FEEL AND KNOW YOUR WORTHINESS

Take a moment to find a quiet spot and close your eyes. Breathe consciously. Go back in time to remember feeling your connection to God at the deepest core of your being.

Remember feeling safe, feeling connected to All That Is, to a place where everything is possible.

Allow your unclouded feeling of sheer joy and bliss to permeate your being as you realize your connection to God. From this place affirm, "I am worthy to receive the bounty and plentitude of Divine Providence and Grace.

Blessings are pouring into my life in every moment. I now receive this bounty and abundance and share this in service.

I thank you now that I feel worthy and deserving of all the gifts that you are providing and that all my needs are met now."

Write down any needs and requests and thank God they now are fulfilled. Amen and So Be It.

Key #19
$Forgiveness$

ALL IS FORGIVEN IN ALL TIME, SPACE, DIMENSIONS, AND ETERNITY

*I*n accessing our intuition, it is important to clear the blocks in the pathway to our inner guidance. Feeling forgiveness helps in clearing the obstacles.

You will begin to see the light and love within everyone as you forgive yourself and others. When we ask to be shown the bigger picture, it unites our consciousness.

Ask to feel compassion so that you can clearly understand why people act out of their wounds. Understand that we are either acting out of love or fear in any given moment. With this understanding, we can see how easy it is to create harm even while not intending to. We become clear channels for Divine Guidance when we feel forgiveness, mercy, and compassion. Forgiveness is a high vibration.

In terms of receiving guidance from your intuition, it is necessary that you are in a high enough energetic frequency to receive it. You can silently ask for forgiveness for yourself and others without directly speaking to the person you perceive as having caused you harm. You can ask that all be restored to harmony in all time, space, dimensions, and eternity while realizing that only the bonds of love remain in eternity.

EXERCISE TO FEEL FORGIVENESS
AND RESTORE PEACE, LOVE AND HARMONY

Find a quiet spot and close your eyes. Breathe consciously.

Call to mind anyone that you hold with unforgiving energy. See this person in your mind's eye as you call upon your Higher Self and their Higher Self. Say or express how you feel. Ask for any unloving energetic cords to be cut. Hold back nothing.

After you have expressed all your feelings, ask that the power of Divine Love heal the situation entirely in all time, space, dimensions and eternity. Understand now that reparation is made in the highest good. You are free from the burden of hate, anger, and resentment that often follow difficult experiences with others.

Ask to see yourself as innocent and loving, creating no harm, and to see the other person the same way. Thank God all has been released to the highest good and only love remains in your experience with this person.

Key #20
Joy

UNABASHED JOY IS YOUR BIRTHRIGHT

*R*emember that everything is energy and vibration. Joy is an energetic vibration that is very high in frequency. Joy does not consider outcomes or attachments to outcome.

Learn to feel unbridled joy for joy's sake. Pay attention to what brings you joy.

Anything we do where we feel obligated to do in any way is not pure joy. Some of our obligations are the result of joyful action. For example, if we write a book, we may need to market it. Remember, in such situations, it is the joy of the action that is important, in this case—writing the book. We can feel joyful about marketing as we align with the higher good of service with our creations.

Joy is your roadmap. Anything you do, and you do with joy, is a roadmap to your life's purpose. Keep following your JOY. Just like gratitude, when you focus on joy, even small joys, the Universe gives back more and more joyful feelings. Joy is a magnet for wonderful experiences to come into your life.

EXERCISE TO BECOME A JOY MAGNET

Find a quiet spot and close your eyes. Breathe consciously as you connect to the joy within you. No matter what you are going through, there is always something to feel joyful about, even if it is just about being alive.

In this moment lies pure potential. Even if you have never felt particularly joyful about your life, here, in this moment, lies the potential to feel pure joy for no reason. There is light and love energy surrounding you in every moment. You are surrounded by your angels and guides. God is within you.

As your mind quiets to this realization, take a moment and begin to imagine the most beautiful, fantastic day of your life. Maybe you are at the beach or receiving an Oscar; with your children or on your bestseller book tour. Take time now to see, feel, and hear everything around your joyful image.

Remember, if you can see it, you can be it. Regular creative visualization will bring these experiences into your life as aligned with the highest good. So keep imagining your joyful life.

Take your journal and begin to record your images and thoughts around your joy. Reread and keep imagining.

Key #21
This is Easier Than I Thought

YOU'RE A NATURAL

When you are living your life's purpose and exploring new things, you will have an experience of *déjà vu* or get a sense that "This is easier than I thought."

You come here to Earth with everything that you need to fulfill your life's purpose. Pay attention to what comes naturally to you. Perhaps you are naturally funny, being kind and compassionate is easy, or you're simply a good listener.

We are all good at different things. In school, it seemed that we had to be good at everything. That is not realistic. We have natural inclinations to what we like and are good at. Pay attention to your inclinations and honor them in yourself. This is not about getting good grades, although you may have—this is about doing and being what you enjoy.

I always loved art. I did not receive great grades in art classes, but knew I loved it. When I paid attention to that, I struck inner gold. What do you love?

EXERCISE FOR DISCOVERING YOUR NATURAL TALENTS

Find a quiet spot and close your eyes. Breathe consciously as you begin to focus on your childhood. Call up a memory when you felt at home, enjoying yourself.

Were you drawn to horses, dogs, cats, or all animals? Did you feel a bond with the animal world? Did you like to play outside, climb trees, or pick flowers? Were you drawn to athletics or dancing, drawing, coloring? Were you quiet or drawn to socialize?

You have unique gifts and talents; many were evident in childhood and then shut down.

Take out your journal and record what you loved to do as a child. You can find a way to incorporate these things into your life now. It's never too late to take that class or workshop and let your inner child play and shine. It's never too late to do what you love. Know that it is important and 100 percent you.

Key #22
Lose Track of Time

YOUR PURPOSE IS TIMELESS

*A*nother key to understanding your life's purpose is feeling outside of time. When you lose track of time doing what you love, you are in the inner world of creation. You are in the present moment, where all potential lies. Watching the clock is a big clue that what you're doing is not your life's purpose. You can lose yourself in tasks like cooking, writing, decorating, or watching something on TV. Anything in which you become engrossed can offer clues to what matters to you. Start noticing where you are losing track of time to uncover more about your life's purpose.

Sometimes it is necessary to hold down that job you don't like. I'll bet that within that finite structure, you can find something to feel "on purpose" about. Over time, I became aware that part of my purpose was to be in service with kindness and compassion. I realized that even when I was waitressing, I could live my purpose by being the very best server I could be. This was regardless of my boss and any corporate rules. I was governed by the spirit within me that was operating on a whole other level. When we immerse ourselves in what we can offer, we can do any job and bring meaning to it.

EXERCISE FOR FINDING THE ETERNAL PART OF YOU THAT IS FREE FROM TIME

Find a quiet spot and close your eyes. Breathe consciously. Focus on your heart center as you ask, "What is it that I am here to bring the world in service? Whether I am running a corporation or sweeping floors, what qualities do I possess that serve on a grander scale? Is it my patience, my love of people or animals, my desire to help, counsel, or teach? Is it my creativity and expression? Is it my sense of humor, compassion or kindness?"

Write down those timeless qualities that you posses and understand when you are in these energies it doesn't matter what time it is or how much time has gone by, you are contributing to the greater good just by being you.

Key #23
That Deep Feeling of Inner Peace

IT PASSETH ALL UNDERSTANDING

As you experience joy, feel a natural ability that does not contain much struggle. Lose yourself in the feeling and notice if you are feeling peace. There is a peace you will feel that is indescribable. It is like the best-kept secret, a mystical enchantment type of inner peace that cannot be destroyed by outside influences. It is yours to keep when nothing else in life is. It is your Soul, your gifts. Your talents are indestructible and last the test of time.

Understand that peace cannot be taken from you; it *is* you. Inner peace is a deep knowing that grows and deepens as you become aligned with who you are and what you are here to do. If you don't know your purpose, look at things that bring you peace.

Have you cooked a wonderful meal for your family and enjoyed the love you have shared? Does this bring you peace? You are a nurturer. You are here to nurture yourself and others.

When you have taken the time to listen to someone fully while being very present and offering your guidance and counsel, does that bring you peace? You are here to counsel and teach.

Do you enjoy walks in nature, the ocean, the mountains, the farmland? Does the Earth bring you peace? You are here to ground energy and radiate strength, as an oak tree does in the forest.

Peace is here now. It is within you and you can connect with it as often as you choose to. Once we connect to our peace it is wonderful to find ways to share it and radiate it into the world.

EXERCISE FOR CONNECTING WITH INNER PEACE

Find a quiet spot and close your eyes. Breathe consciously. Breathe Peace in, Breathe Peace out. Feel the rhythm of continuous peace flowing in and out of you.

Quiet your mind as you allow stray thoughts to surface. Watch them but do not become engaged with them. Under the thoughts lies your deep inner peace, calm as stilled water, like glass. That is the real you.

Take a moment and feel the peace of this moment as you connect with the deepest part of you which is peace.

Peace has no agenda. Peace is still. Peace is your connection to your Higher Self that knows that everything is always OK.

You are already whole. Imagine the path of your life as a spiral leading to the core of who you are. This is your True Self. Your True Self is not affected by the outside world. It is ever peaceful and ever joyful. An awareness of this is a key to real happiness.

Taking your journal out, begin to write down your experience of peace. Ask your Higher Self what activities remind you of this deep peace.

$\mathcal{K}ey$ #24
$\mathcal{P}ay \mathcal{A}ttention$

THE UNIVERSE IS TALKING TO YOU

*A*s you go through your day, your week, your year, your life—pay attention. Your life's purpose is continually evolving and making itself known. Joy is your roadmap to the greatest destination, your whole life. Your life is a journey and if we knew all at once our gifts, the journey would not be necessary.

Pay attention to clues, signs, and synchronicity from the Universe. There are no coincidences. Pay attention to what people say; listen with your whole heart and do not make up your responses in advance. Even "your enemy" may offer clues. This is an exaggerated way to say—do not discount where you hear the Voice of God. Learn to listen with neutral, nonjudgmental ears.

Use discernment. God speaks through all of us. Pay attention to what makes you feel inspired.

I learned about signs when I became a Certified Angel Messenger. I took a class and learned how to connect with the angels. It was the beginning of an exciting psychic, intuitive career for me. I regularly ask for signs. I also pay attention to what I see and hear around me.

Here's an example: Years ago, I was looking for a new job. I prayed and intended it to be so. I began to notice ads on TV for this place of employment I had never known about. I received the sign to go there and apply; I did and got hired on the spot. We can receive messages through ads on TV, songs on the radio, or even billboards. There is a spiritual aspect to life, that when we tune into it, it is always spot on.

My favorite "ask-for-a-sign" moment was when I was driving through New York City asking for a sign for my television show. I heard in my intuition "Lucky Star." I thought, "That's a Madonna song, I have a 5-hour drive; I'll find it on the radio." I then looked up and the biggest bus I'd ever seen, sporting a huge sign on the back, that said it all: The Lucky Star Bus, Boston-New York! As you can probably guess, I heard Madonna's *Lucky Star* song as I turned onto my street. The Universe was speaking and I was listening.

EXERCISE TO TUNE INTO THE SIGNS OF THE UNIVERSE

Find a quiet spot and close your eyes. Breathe consciously. Begin to quiet your mind as you ask your Higher Self to guide you and thank it for helping you see clear signs now. "Thank you, Higher Self, for your connection to the Universe and All That Is."

See yourself going about your day, noticing the signs that you are on the right track. Notice conversations around you, songs on the radio, and ads on TV that you hear and see repeatedly. Often, signs come in threes. The Universe is always showing you the way and speaking to you.

Ask for signs and then let go of how you will receive them. You will feel a light-hearted, magical way of living as you connect with the signs from the Universe and your angels that are all around you.

Take out your journal and write down any questions that you would like to see answered. Write down any signs from your intuition to watch for. And so it is.

Key #25
You Have a Higher Self

IT KNOWS EVERYTHING

You have a Higher Self; it knows you like no other. It is connected to God and Higher Truth and is always available to you. It is the highest aspect of your Soul . Some refer to it as their Guardian Angel.

Your Higher Self knows your easiest path in life. It understands your deepest fears and your loftiest aspirations. When you learn to listen to this voice, your life will be forever changed for the better. That is, if you do indeed wish to enjoy a life of ease and grace.

When you want to connect with the Higher Self, simply call on it. You are always being guided by your Higher Self, but sometimes it is difficult to hear. Start by calling on your Higher Self. You can receive answers in writing or by speaking it out loud.

EXERCISE FOR HEARING YOUR HIGHER SELF

Begin with a prayer:

I call on white-gold light to surround myself; I call on my Higher Self. Thank you that I am protected while I am channeling. I ask that the highest good come through, highest and best, better than I could ever imagine. I thank you that I channel with clarity and purity today. Thank you God, Amen.

Take out your journal and begin to ask questions and write down the answers. You can also ask questions out loud and speak the answers that come to you. You can ask questions about your relationships to a partner, yourself, children, friends or God.

After you say your prayer and ask your question, pause and notice any feelings. Those are your spiritual gift of clairsentience. Do you notice any *knowing* about your answer to the question? That is claircognizance. Notice what you hear. That is clairaudience. Notice any images in your mind's eye. That is clairvoyance.

Whatever you feel, know, hear or see, begin to write without editing yourself. You may begin with Dearest (your name) and your Higher Self will speak to you by name. You can speak out loud exactly what you hear without editing.

If you have questions about relationships begin with this prayer:

I call on white gold light to surround myself; I call on my Higher Self. Thank you that I am protected while I am channeling. I ask that the highest good come through, highest and best better than I could ever imagine. I thank you that I channel with clarity and purity today. Thank you God, Amen. Please answer this question about my relationship: Dearest (your name here) now write in your journal or speak out loud what you hear.

You can ask your Higher Self about anything. Along with relationships, it knows about your career, life's purpose, and emotional well-being. You have this inner guidance for your life like no other. As you practice connecting to your Higher Self and receive answers, you will never rely on the opinions of others again.

You are in the driver's seat of your life, living your highest good when you listen and follow the guidance of your Higher Self.

Key #26
Detoxify Your Body

CLEAN YOUR INNER HOUSE

As spiritual beings in physical bodies, it can be easy to not take the very best care of ourselves. Why is that?

The body is self-healing in many ways. It may take a while for us to notice that we may have been running on empty, burning the candle at both ends, smoking too many cigarettes, or drinking too much coffee. Toxins take time to accumulate and we may not notice the steady and increasing negative consequences right away. What we consume into our beings does matter.

It's always good to check with your doctor about the best choices for you. Also check with a good professional medical intuitive. A medical intuitive can tell you specifically what you may be allergic to and what the best foods are for you.

There is no cookie-cutter diet. Food affects everyone differently. I have found that paying attention to what I eat and drink has made a great difference in my energy levels and overall feeling of well-being. I don't recommend a particular detox or diet program. I do recommend that you pay attention not only to what you are consuming, but also what you use to clean your environment, put on your skin, and so on. Toxins will overload you eventually. Toxic overload compromises your health and ability to live your purpose with passion, zest, and energy.

EXERCISE TO CONNECT WITH YOUR PHYSICAL WELL-BEING

Find a quiet spot and close your eyes. Breathe consciously, feeling your body fill up with life-affirming and Spirit-connecting oxygen. Breathe deeply and feel yourself fully connected to Spirit with your breath. Call on your Higher Self and ask, "What kind of changes do I need to make in my diet and environment? I am now choosing to provide the best nutrition and healthiest environment for the temple of God that I am. Help me find the information that will serve me, as I am like no other. Tell me now what the highest good choices are for me in terms of food and drink. Do I need more greens? Filtered water? Organic fruits and vegetables?"

See your body and home clear and toxin free. What does that look like? What does that feel like? Write down your answers in your journal. When you begin to detoxify your home and yourself, you will feel more clear, light and free and you will be able to hear your intuition more clearly.

Key #27
The Emotional Realm

GET OUT THE TISSUE

We have an emotional body that is the keeper of our raw, pure emotions. Many of us were not taught to express these emotions healthfully or otherwise. Why is honoring and processing our emotions important regarding intuition and life's purpose? Well, remember everything we experience is in our Wealth Centers—the good, the bad, and the ugly. Just because we are not shouting our hurt and pain from the rooftops doesn't mean we aren't shouting it into the ethers. Everything is energy, including our emotions. If we don't deal with them, they deal with us.

It is a good idea to notice that we have emotions, such as joy, sorrow, fear, and love. These emotional states are different from the pure beings of love and joy we are. Our beings, when connected to love and joy, remain constant. Our emotions, when connected to love and joy, fluctuate. Emotions are reactive to our external surroundings, our being is not.

We all have powerful emotions. If they become repressed and stifled, we suffer. If we express them in an unhealthy manner, we create suffering and then suffer ourselves. Understand that emotions are clues to where we are wounded. Emotions need to be expressed. Emotions need to be honored for the gateway of information they provide. Emotions should not be judged; they simply are. Emotions can be expressed healthfully.

Creativity will help you release and transform negative emotions. Get out the tissues and cry. Feel your feelings, acknowledge them. You deserve to be heard. You have an inner child within who needs to express the emotions you may have bottled up for years.

We are all feeling beings. Understand that emotions can feel overwhelming. Many boys are taught not to cry. I encourage the release of emotions in safe ways because all emotions carry energy.

If you are not expressing yourself in a healthy way, you will carry these negative energies within you, whether you are aware of it or not. You will be triggered by other people when you don't deal with your emotions. When others push your buttons, they are triggering your bottled up emotions. That can be a painful experience. Often someone will trigger our emotions because, deep down, the actions or words remind us of an old wound. This person did not create the wound, but here we are reacting to it now because we never dealt the emotions from the original wound.

I recommend eliminating your buttons by loving yourself and letting your emotions surface. The only emotions that can hurt you are the ones that you don't express and release.

Expressing your emotions through anger is not what I am talking about. Anger is just a stifled emotion that comes out unconsciously and creates harm.

Understand that your emotions are yours. No one can truly push your buttons once you understand your own emotional states.

EXERCISE TO CLEAR YOUR EMOTIONAL BODY

Find a quiet spot and close your eyes. Breathe consciously. Call on your Higher Self and ask to be shown areas in your emotional body that can be healed.

Many events and experiences in our lives have created emotional attachments. Ask to be shown an emotional area that has been hidden from you, so that you now can safely release this pain. As you recall any painful memories, ask that Spirit transform them into Love.

If it's sadness, feel it, cry, and then thank your inner child for releasing this sadness now. You are the spiritual grown-up here. Help your inner child safely release painful emotions. Understand that you have always done your best and everyone in your life has been doing the best he or she can as well. Acknowledge your feelings and honor what comes up.

Write in your journal anything that comes up for you around emotions that surface. Writing as a practice will help you release your emotions effectively. Do not carry them in your body. You are a being of Divine Expression. You can use your emotions to channel your creativity and turn emotional challenges of doubt and fear into Faith, Hope, and Love.

Key #28
$Connect$ $with$ $Your$ $Spirit$

IT'S NOT GOING ANYWHERE

*U*nderstand that you are an eternal being. You are infinite in your potential.

We all have egos. The job of the ego is to try to protect us from painful experiences. Your spirit feels no pain and has no need for protection. Pure love radiating from your Spirit is the most powerful force in the Universe. Pure love has no need to be concerned about karma or revenge or harm caused to it. These all come from our egos. On this physical plane we have time. We have responsibilities.

You have a Spirit within you that exists in timeless dimensions. What does that mean for you here and now? You can connect to the True Self, the True Spirit, within you at any time and feel the burdens of everyday life lift. Your Spirit is Light; it is in constant joy, peace, and bliss.

The right hemisphere of your brain is connected to All That Is. You can tap into the Infinite Potential and Divine Mind of God. It is who you are, now and always. It has solutions to your problems and answers to your questions. It has unlimited creativity that will serve you and others. It doesn't need a reason to be happy. It *is* pure happiness. It exists free from attachment and outcome.

EXERCISE TO CONNECT WITH YOUR SPIRIT

Find a quiet spot and close your eyes. Begin breathing consciously. Once you are breathing deeply, ask your Spirit to come forth. Feel the vibrancy, potency, and living expression of God within you. Connect with the part of you that is always OK, has all the answers, and feels no pain. It does not judge and has no fear. It sheds light on all your situations and experiences.

By connecting with it now, you feel comforted, stable, and strong. You are *in* the world, but not *of* the world. You are timeless, you are free. You are in a constant state of joy, peace, and bliss as you connect to your Spirit.

From this place, you can choose loving experiences, and feel grace and flow. The highest good flows through you, as like attracts like. You are now able to see the highest good for your life.

As you connect with your Spirit and its infinite love and sense of well-being, ask it if there is anything that is no longer serving you. Ask if you need to let go of anything. Ask to be shown the clearest path for your life's purpose.

Are there lingering heavy emotions that need to be cleared and purged? Forgive yourself and others in all time, space, dimensions, and eternity. If you feel anything less than pure love for yourself and others, absolve them now.

As you connect with your Spirit, the False self may appear. Pure Love is the way of Spirit. Anything different that you experienced in the past or are experiencing now can be let go with this new understanding. You are a spark from the Creator of Worlds. All that is created from love is here for you now. It is not necessary to experience anything different. Compassion and understanding from your Spirit is the Truth that will set you free.

Write in your journal anything that comes up to be released and transmuted with the love of your Spirit now. Write down the feelings of bliss. Describe your feelings as you connect to this Great Spirit within you.

Key #29
Listen To Your Spirit

TAME YOUR TO-DO LIST

Years ago, in an unconscious state of mind, I prided myself on how booked my calendar was or how many tasks were on my to-do list. I enjoyed the great feeling of accomplishment as I checked things off my list, as if that were some sort of representation of how important I was.

That type of thinking led to inevitable burnout. My body fell into a depression that forced me to clear everything from my calendar. It was a scary time. Coming back from that emotional, mental, physical, and spiritual ground zero took some doing. The good news is that through spiritual practice, I came back stronger than ever.

I developed a clear and balanced perspective that now allows my Spirit to guide my day. My calendar is full enough and I have plenty to do on my list. The difference now, though, is that I depend on my inner Self, my Spirit, to connect me to what is truly important. I no longer need to feel busy to feel needed or important.

We have a finite amount of time in the day and it is easy to feel overwhelmed. We all have a certain amount of must-do responsibilities, like going to work, bill paying, taking care of our families, and on and on. If we don't pay attention to what our Spirit is telling us, we may be wasting our precious time with distractions. We may miss out on fulfilling and meaningful ways to spend our time.

Are you on your own to do list? Do you make time for yourself, your spiritual practice? Do you know that the way you spend your time can contribute to a feeling of well-being or stress in your life? How do you discern the best use of your time on any given day?

My Spirit is the part of me that knows no bounds or limitations, that knows the answers in the highest good to my questions. Recently, I meditated and asked my Spirit, "With all I've got on my plate, what is the best use of my time today?" I was surprised at the answer. I heard, "Take care of yourself, your children, your husband, and your home."

I thought, "Really? That's it? What about my book, my work?"

"Let it be," I heard. "First things first."

I realized in that moment that often, I had put myself last. While being an entrepreneur required time and effort, so did my life. It was a revelation to realize that cleaning my home could be a spiritual practice. Taking care of myself, my family, and my home felt simple and complete.

My Spirit showed me that taking care of the very foundation of my life was a great place from which to launch. I needed to take care of my foundation, and then manage my day with renewed priorities. Many of us are here to save the world, but we need to save ourselves first.

EXERCISE TO LISTEN TO YOUR SPIRIT AND DISCERN YOUR DAILY PRIORITIES

Find a quiet spot and close your eyes. Breathe consciously as you connect to your Spirit. Your Spirit, the timeless you, knows the best use of your time. Think about everything that you think you have to do this day.

Understand that Rome was not built in a day. What you do today will be the foundation of tomorrow. You have all the time you need to complete what is truly important. God does not give us more than we can handle.

See in your mind's eye your list of tasks one by one. Give them your full attention. As everything has energy, including your to-do list. Begin to feel in your body a positive feeling or negative feeling with each item. We all have basic, go-to-work, must-do responsibilities we need to do to survive. Besides those survival tasks, feel the energy of each item on your list. You know exactly how to make the best use of your time. Watch as you try to filter the information with excuses like, "I'll do that later" or "that's not important enough."

Our minds and logic are not the best navigators for our life. Our feelings are. Ask your Self, "What is truly important for me to do today? Not tomorrow, today. Is it rest? Is it mundane chores? Is it grocery shopping or applying for a new job?"

Pay attention to the feelings within you. You will notice a calm peace when you suggest your highest good, even if it doesn't make sense. Clean your house instead of creating a new website? The answer could be yes. Clearing your space could increase the flow of energy through your home and allow the creative energy to gather more easily for you. We don't logically know the answers, but our Spirit does.

Take a moment and write in your journal what is the best use of your time today in the highest good. Listen to your Spirit—it won't steer you wrong!

Key #30
Feed Your Spirit

YOUR FIVE-STAR SPIRITUAL RESTAURANT

We have heard by the very word of God that man does not live on bread alone. What does this mean regarding the feeding of your Spirit? When I say to feed your Spirit, I am asking you to consider that you have a Spirit within you. Your Spirit relishes the ability to express its Divine Creative Expression in the world. You are born with unique gifts and talents and you are here to express them with joy. We each have a purpose. We are all unique in our energy signature and expression. That is great news, as there truly is no competition in the spiritual world.

In the higher realms, we are recognized and celebrated for our uniqueness. Most of us did not grow up with this concept. In school, it felt as though we all had to be good at math, English, or art. We were all expected to perform to a standard that was created out of competition and making people feel less-than.

I was one of those students. I felt fairly brilliant, but failed to make that impression on my teachers. I was told I was not doing the art projects in class correctly. This feeling of not being good enough affected me for years. The breakthrough I had later in life, when I bought paints and painted from my heart, changed everything. I loved to paint whether my art teacher in high school thought I was any good or not. I began to feed my Spirit with what brought me feelings of joy, meaning, and inner success.

I love to coach all forms of creativity, as creativity is a golden gateway to feeding your Spirit. There are no rules. You can paint outside the lines when you feed your spirit with creative nourishment.

Another example of creativity is people who describe themselves as "foodies." While preparing a meal from a recipe is very rewarding, imagine throwing in your own ingredients and improvising a bit. I advocate breaking free from traditional limitations that have told us things must be done a certain way. I am not talking about law-abiding rules here. Just look for ways in your day to feed the creative genius in your Soul .

Great musicians do this all the time. I loved my Elton John records growing up. When I saw him play in a live concert, I experienced a whole new level of his music. I watched and listened to him break free from even his own established recordings and belt out his songs with passion. In the moment, he made creative changes to his already unique style. He changed chords and tones with abandon.

You can feel this in-the-moment, creative-genius energy. You are the Master Creator of your life. You are a genius of your own gifts and talents.

Don't let conventional thinking make you believe you are less than great. Don't discredit your brilliance because someone else says so. It's never too late to acknowledge your creative genius, your snowflake print on the world like no other. You are here to shine and share all that you are. All of your greatness is like no other.

EXERCISE TO FEED AND NOURISH YOUR SPIRIT

Find a quiet spot and close your eyes. Breathe consciously. Feel the connection to the deepest eternal aspect of yourself. Ask to be shown the higher awareness of what will bring your Spirit nourishment.

Forgive yourself for working too hard and ignoring yourself. Feel the feelings of knowing that you are here to be cared for, loved, and nourished by your own Soul .

Your Soul knows how to care for your Spirit. They are acting and governed by the higher laws, not those of man. Your Soul and Spirit are in alignment. With cooperation of the Universal laws, Soul and Spirit will provide lasting happiness and peace. As you master your Soul's lesson and purpose, and fully engage your Spirit, you will grow and evolve at an accelerated rate, while bringing much joy and service into the world.

That is why, Dear One, you must discern and distinguish between what is feeding your Spirit and what is feeding your ego. Mastering that distinction will allow you to flourish on every level and in every facet of your life.

How do you discern which jaws of the hungry lion you are feeding? Your Spirit is fed by God alone and through that connection, nothing outside of you, including your accomplishments, can ever fulfill you. When you are truly feeding your Spirit, you are not thinking about the outcome of your tasks. It is pure joy in the moment of creating, without any consideration or thought of what it means on a material level.

You've heard the saying, "Dance as if no one is watching." Martina McBride has a beautiful song, *Anyway. The Paradoxical Commandments* by Kent Keith say "Love anyway. Love no matter the cost or if you get it back."

Ask to be shown in the most basic and simple ways, what feeds and nourishes your being. Your connection to

Divine Spirit through meditation, awareness, or contemplation will always bring you closer to your own Spirit.

You are eternally connected to All That Is. As the unique snowflake of conscious being you are, ask to be shown ways in which you can fulfill this very primary directive of feeding and nourishing yourself. Does it require more one-on-one time with God, the Creator?

Deepening this connection is a big key to feeding your Spirit. Know this: all aspirations that bring forth love you can feel in your Soul will feed your Spirit.

Write in your journal ways that come to you now to feed your Spirit. Don't edit or judge. Dance and write like no one is watching.

Key #31
Your Intuitive Channels

CLAIRSENTIENCE – YOU CAN FEEL IT

I have studied intuition to a certain degree. It is a spiritual gift that we are all born with. I also acknowledge that we can develop this gift through study and practice. We are not left orphaned in this world to fend for ourselves. God truly gives us the keys to the Kingdom. Through the various means, it is up to us and our free will to own our gifts, our power, and our connection to the cosmic consciousness that contains all the answers to our questions. It is up to us to own our gifts and use them for the highest good for ourselves and others.

What does intuition feel like? There are four main channels and once we understand how they work within us, navigating them is a lot easier. *Clairsentience,* or feeling the answers, is one of our Divine birthrights.

What does "feel the answers" to your questions mean? You have been aware of gut feelings. You have felt butterflies in your stomach, or gotten sick to your stomach as you think of an unpleasant experience. Understand that the connection between Mind, Body, and Spirit is real.

Feelings start with paying attention to the physical feelings in your body, like rapid heartbeat or stomach upset. Feelings of Truth can resonate with a peace and calm like no other. You have an inner GPS in feeling the energetic make up of your physical body. Feelings and your body cannot lie.

The key is distinguishing true feelings from false ones. Feelings of fear exist, feelings of doubt exist. The exercise below is designed to help you distinguish the Truth of your feelings as it relates to intuition. As a professional psychic reader, I rely on my true feelings to guide me and my clients.

EXERCISE TO CONNECT WITH YOUR INNER GPS, YOUR TRUE FEELINGS

Take a moment to find a quiet space, close your eyes, and breathe consciously. Feel the connection with your breath as you ask your Higher Self to guide you in this meditation.

Ask a question to which you would like an answer and begin to notice the feelings in your physical body before you hear the answer in your mind. Do you feel uptight, nervous, or do you feel at ease with the answer?

We receive very clear information from our deepest feelings at the most basic, rawest level. Understand that human fear and other emotions can cloud our inner feeling GPS, which is why it is important to ask our questions, feel our feelings, and allow unclouded information to come through us.

If we ask a question and feel we may lose our job, of course we will "feel" fear. This exercise is a way to feel your answers without the fear, so you ask and feel gut reactions.

The difference in feeling the Truth of what to do comes with discerning the feelings. For instance, you ask "Am I going to lose my job?" and the answer is "Yes," you will feel that uncomfortable feeling in your stomach, but don't stop there. Within the highest realms is always the answer to your prayers, so you feel that and then you ask another question. "What will replace this sick feeling I feel?"

Understand with Divine Providence, for every door that closes, a new door opens. When you feel uncomfortable feelings in your body, keep asking good questions with the faith, hope, love, and trust that your best interest is in the interest of God, the Creator.

When I work with clients, there may be "bad" news, but we don't stop there—nor should you. You are here to experience your highest good. Challenges will come along. Tune in and ask your Higher Self to show you, with feeling, where you will land if you feel the earth below you is shaky.

If you feel fear in your body, feel it, but don't stop there. Remember Faith, Hope, and Love are real and yours. Ask your feeling Self how to get from Fear A to Love Z. It knows the answer. For every wall you hit, there is a corner to turn. Use your feelings as guideposts, but do not let them lead you astray. Know your spiritual rights and truths as resonating with abundance, joy, peace, and love. Feel and know that you can ask and realign in every moment to the Truth of this understanding.

Feelings of fear feel real, but they are *not* real. Only love is real. If you feel anything less than that, understand that you can find your way back. It is your right and who you are to live without fear and feel complete joy.

Ask your Higher Self to guide, inform, and counsel you on ways to feel and navigate your way with the peace, hope, love, and compassion that is yours.

Take out your journal and ask your Self what feeling is guiding you now to make changes in your life. Are you dissatisfied with your job, love life, relationships in general? Is your health an issue? Write down your true feelings about each one.

As you feel less-than-positive experiences and gut reactions, remind yourself that your True Self only feels the highest good. Write down the positive aspects of feeling your gut feelings, as though you are being shown how to change these influences in your life into the greater good.

There is no challenge that God cannot meet and transform. There is no fear that love cannot heal. There is no reason to feel worry when trust and faith are in place. You have this spiritual gift of True feeling to override whatever false feeling you ever had in this lifetime. Feel and write about your true feelings of hope and answers for your life now. Connect to this great spiritual feeling aspect of yourself.

Key #32
Your Intuitive Channels

CLAIRCOGNIZANCE –
I JUST KNOW IT/I DON'T KNOW ANYTHING

*A*long with feeling our intuition, sometimes we can just "know something." We do not have to have read it in a textbook or heard it on the news. We all have an intuitive channel called *claircognizance* that just knows the highest good and answers for our lives, without knowing how we know.

I often tell clients that I don't know anything. What I mean is that when you work with me, you will not get my opinion or anything I ever read in a book about your situation. You will get 100-percent intuitive information. Answers feel like they drop in from the heavens. There is no logical explanation to why I know what I know for my clients. Time-tested accuracy and repeat clients tell me, along with my own knowing, I know things I have no way of knowing. I know them with this psychic intuitive ability.

There is a way of being I maintain in my daily life that allows this other-worldly, supernatural information to come to me. I let go of the need to know things in a literal sense. I let go of the need to be right. I acknowledge the field of existence that tells me there is something greater than myself—my "small self," that is. I allow my great Self to meld with the greater good and higher understanding. As I allow this relationship, acknowledge it, and intend it be so, I am filled with a knowing beyond logical comprehension.

I also empty my cup, so to speak, so that I may be filled with the Higher wisdom. I no longer act with my free will, as though I know every answer to every question. I am not a "know-it-all" — we're all familiar with that type of energy. Rather, I empty all former preconceptions of what I think I know when I ask for information for myself and others. I do not have an answer ready-made or already formulated. I am an empty vessel and a channel working with the Higher Realms.

When I ask a question, I am free from opinions and textbook theory. I open and allow all information in the highest good to flow through me; the results are nothing short of miraculous. This is what it is like to know something. To know you receive information from the higher realms and your Higher Self is nothing like receiving information from someone's filtered experience. You can't logically explain how you know intuitive information.

This is an excellent spot to caution against being a psychic voyeur. We, as being in full integrity with our intuition, do not look into people and what they are going through and decide to tell them what we know. That would be a violation of free will. We do not snoop into anyone's life, period. We do not presume to know about other people. The gift of knowing is for ourselves and clients from whom we gain permission to receive this clarity. We do not want to be a bunch of psychic know-it-alls. That proves nothing. These spiritual gifts are to be used with the noblest of intentions. With great service in mind, there is no end to the knowledge we can experience on a whole other level.

EXERCISE FOR CONNECTING WITH YOUR INNATE KNOWING

Find a quiet spot and close your eyes. Breathe consciously as you connect with your inner knowing. Call on your Higher Self and begin to feel and know the answers to your questions. Ask yourself any question now.

Oftentimes, our egos will say we don't have the answers to our questions. As spiritual beings, we *do* know the answers.

If you feel a block when you ask your question, then ask, "If I did know the answer, what would it be?" It's often possible to sideline the ego by saying this. You may hear "I don't know." Follow it with, "OK, but if I did know, what would I say?" The highest good answers are always within us.

You also need to let go of a particular answer. Stay open. Empty your cup of what you think the answer should be. Get out of the way and allow your deep knowing to share itself with you.

One of the primary blocks to hearing information from the Higher realms, including your Higher Self, is that you are afraid of the answer. Deep down, it might make you uncomfortable when you hear that changes in your life are in order for the highest good. I have taught myself to stay very open and fear nothing when I ask for information. Courage and faith are required to hear and not block what you are receiving. Stay open when you ask for intuitive insight.

Please get out your journal and write down what you know to be true. You know a lot. Know that God does not give you any information that you can't handle. Stay open and allow your inner knowingness to come through.

Key #33
Your Intuitive Channels

CLAIRAUDIENCE —
I HEAR YOU LOUD AND CLEAR

*T*he next channel of Divine guidance is *clairaudience*. I often tell clients that part of their life's purpose is something they are already doing.

I am a professional coach and spiritual counselor. I spent many years in apprenticeship to hone my skills and fine tune my abilities. I always loved to help my friends and anyone who would come to me looking for advice. I gave this freely and from my heart. I could, and did, spend hours on the phone helping friends with their problems. I do the same thing now — professionally. See how my hobby turned into a career?

I will never forget when the clairaudient channel (which means "clear hearing") opened up for me. I was helping a friend with heartbreak from her relationship. I was talking as usual and then all of a sudden, it seemed I had another voice much like my own, but more powerful and knowing. That other voice began to tell me what was really happening with her situation. When I told her the insight I was receiving, she exclaimed "You are spot-on with that, Anne!" It was a curious bit of new hearing I had discovered, this voice that provided amazing answers and insights, and was always accurate.

Over the years, I have learned to trust this voice above all others. As a gift, it is a priceless pearl. You have this gift as well. The clairaudient channel is something you can develop.

As a professional intuitive, I have learned ways to access this voice of my Higher Self. When I work with clients, I also call on their Higher Self, Masters of Light such as Jesus and Buddha, and sometimes Archangels and other Ascended beings. Always, the combined voice of this celestial team is wise, knowing, loving, peaceful, and understanding. It is also powerful and will not mince words. If you are open to hearing this guidance, it is life changing. You can always distinguish Divine guidance from ego or spirits, because of its high vibration and the quality of information that resonates with spiritual laws. You can feel it.

To tune into this very high and fine frequency, it is necessary to vibrate close to the same frequency. If you have any fear, anger, doubt, or resentment, you will be vibrating at too low a level to even hear this guidance.

Go to a frequency of love if you have fear around something about which you are seeking an answer. Let it go for now. Do your best to feel peace and love. Have faith that the best outcome is in your highest good. Then ask your questions. You must shift your thoughts and feelings to a higher vibration to get accurate answers.

When I work with people, I hear some traumatizing things. I cannot allow myself to feel anything less than love or I cannot help them. I cannot cry and sympathize, as that makes my vibration too low, which prevents higher-level guidance from coming through. It takes practice; understand you can receive accurate information from your intuitive channels.

EXERCISE FOR HEARING YOUR DIVINE GUIDANCE

Find a quiet spot and close your eyes. Breathe consciously as you focus on your inner being and calmly call forth your Higher Self.

Say "Thank you, God, that I am in a protected space. I now experience my highest and best, better than I could ever imagine. Thank you, God. I am a clear and pure channel for myself today."

Think of a question you would like answered. Remember to stay out of the way. Drop your expectations of what kind of answer you will receive. Stay open. If you are worried or nervous about the answer, acknowledge this and then affirm, "I am open to my highest good."

Take out your journal and begin to pay attention to any voice within you that sounds like yours, except it is unquestionably loving, wise and knowing. Feel the love, gratitude and appreciation you feel for being able to hear this voice. What you put your attention on expands so think positive loving thoughts of gratitude. Write down anything that comes to you from this voice of Love within your Soul .

Key #34
Your Intuitive Channels

CLAIRVOYANCE –
I CAN SEE CLEARLY NOW

*I*t is my wish that you are seeing more and more how much intuitive power and information you have available to you. The last channel I will be discussing is the channel of *clairvoyance*, or clear seeing.

All of us understand what it's like to see something in our mind's eye. We all have imagination and can see or daydream and think nothing of it. Clairvoyance is understanding that you can be *shown* answers to your questions. You can be shown your purpose as well.

My first experience of seeing my own clairvoyant ability was when I was shown in my mind's eye one of my paintings with words around it. I didn't do readings at the time, so I didn't understand that the picture in my mind was a psychic channel. I saw an image of my painting and words around it. I asked myself, "Is this a book?" I heard "Yes, you will write a book." I just about fell over, but all at once, I could see my first book and knew the message was true. I did write that book and it does have the painting with words around it.

When working with clients, I am often shown images to better describe to my client what is happening. It is said that a picture is worth a thousand words, and oftentimes, it is. I get so much information from a picture in my mind shown to me by the guides and Masters I am working with.

Recently, while working with a client, I was shown a woman wearing layers and layers of sweaters and coats. I asked what that meant and the guides told me it was a representation of her trying to protect herself from the cold and arctic climate. However, it was summer at the time and she was still being dragged down with all those layers. The message was for her to let go of things she no longer needed. It was time to get rid of the wool coats. They had served her previously, but she no longer needed them. The message was that she could adapt more easily now. It was time to let go of former programming telling her that she needed more protection. That programming was outdated. She could be in a new environment now and thrive.

The Higher realms are great at showing us visual images to help us in our lives. Understand that God did not leave us without great gifts. I believe the greatest gifts are our spiritual gifts. The Kriya Yoga meditation I described in Key #14 opened up my clairvoyant channel. All art, as sacred image, helps to get you into your right brain and expand your creative, intuitive abilities.

EXERCISE FOR CLEAR SEEING
AND EXPANDED INNER VISION

Find a quiet spot and close your eyes. Breathe consciously as you begin to focus on the place between your eyebrows, known as the third eye of intuition. Focus. Gaze inward, focusing on this central point between your brows.

Notice any colors or points of light swirling. Allow yourself to relax and remain free from trying to see anything. Just keep your eyes closed and honor your inner vision.

Call on the Holy Spirit to now heal, clear and activate your third eye of intuition. Notice any warmth you may feel at that spot. Affirm to the Universe, "I am willing to see what I need to see and know what I need to know for my highest good."

Just as with the other channels, a willingness to be open and free from fear is necessary to channel higher guidance and clear seeing.

Know that clear seeing can come to you with your eyes open as well. Be aware of images in your mind that speak to you. Your Higher Self, Guides, and Angels will speak to you in the language with which you are most familiar.

Know also that all sacred images enhance your ability to see clearly with your intuition. Visit museums, watch movies, work with oracle cards, paint, or draw. Really look around you and see your environment. Notice everything.

Take your journal out now and write down anything that you see in your mind's eye. It could be colors, symbols or images and understand that they have meaning for you.

Key #35
Grounding

REACH FOR THE STARS
AND KEEP YOUR FEET ON THE GROUND

For the longest time, I heard about grounding. It felt very foreign to me as a concept. In the metaphysical community, you hear over and over how important it is to ground yourself. As creative beings, many of us like to live in our heads and not so much in our bodies. It is blissful to think and daydream about great ideas.

The problem is that many people think about becoming writers, but they don't actually sit down and write. Many people don't do what it takes to turn their writing dream into a reality. This is true for all great ideas and concepts. How many times have you seen a great invention come along and heard someone say "I could have thought of that." Well, you could have, but you didn't. Often, that person may have gotten the idea and done nothing about it.

We need to take these God-given ideas and ground them into reality. A book or any other great idea does not come to fruition without a process for bringing it into being. Let's discuss grounding, manifesting and turning a great idea into something concrete.

Turning the nonphysical into the physical begins with grounding. Grounding refers to feeling solid in your physical body. You are not living in your head, with that floaty, out-of-body feeling we all experience from time to time. I am talking about being in the here and now and being aware of your body and physical environment. It is a place of present awareness. Think of the difference between the person who *says* he or she wants to write a book, and the one who actually does?

The following exercise shows you some ways to be the vehicle for Divine ideas and inspirations you are meant to be. God works through us. Spirit can be made manifest and we are the conduits. We have the physical bodies to carry forth the Divine expressions and means to express God here and now. This is Heaven on Earth.

EXERCISE FOR GROUNDING

Here are some simple techniques that you can use to ground yourself. I am not going to ask you to close your eyes, but rather, to find a quiet spot and breathe consciously.

Focusing on your breath for several minutes is one way to ground yourself. Being grounded requires that you are very present in the moment. As you begin to focus on your breathing, also notice your heartbeat. Feel the peace in this moment. In this moment, there is nothing else.

Look at your hands. Notice your fingernails or any rings you are wearing. Are your nails well groomed? Signs of not being grounded can show up in our physical appearance and becomes evident in the way we are paying attention to ourselves. Are your fingernails filed and clean, manicured, attractive? If not, have you been living in your head with other things to do? This is just one gentle reminder that says you are here in a physical body now and you need to pay attention to it.

Look around the room or space you are in right now? Is it picked up and clutter free? Look deeply around your environment and you can see how present you are to your life. Is there dust you have been overlooking? There is no judgment here; this exercise is about bringing you into harmony with your body and physical surroundings. Mundane chores provide grounding.

We must accept that here on earth, houses do not clean themselves. It can be spiritual to clean your house, cook nourishing food, chop wood, or carry water. You can hug a tree, walk on the grass, kiss your children, and hug your spouse. Anything that reminds you that you are a physical being, and at the same time, a spiritual being, will help ground you. Being grounded will help in bringing forth your purpose, dreams, and visions.

Take out your journal and write about your findings with the above exercise. As you ground, you will reach for the stars and fly.

Key #36
Ideas

THE LIGHT BULB GOES ON

After you experience what it feels like to be very present in your body and environment, begin to notice ideas that come to you. Brilliant, God-given ideas feel noble —and they are. When you begin to resonate with a higher frequency, you will receive great ideas.

When I work with clients, I am often a receiver of great ideas for them. Then we begin the process of turning these great ideas into something concrete, such as a workshop, website, book, or anything else physical. We are co-creators with God. We have the ability to create anything in our lives.

With free will, we are free to create a mess. There is no judgment with that. We can align our will with God's will and create from that place if we choose to experience the most harmonious experiences in our lives. It is our choice.

Ideas are not things you can stalk or find—they come to you. I have found it helpful to sincerely state to the Universe, "I am in alignment with my highest good. I am open to receiving Divine ideas."

You are in your own Divine power to receive brilliant ideas when you are vibrating with the frequencies of joy, gratitude, unconditional love, and faith. No matter what is happening in your life, find a way to feel these Divine frequencies. Even the littlest thing can shift your energy to receive these abundant ideas.

The following exercise is a prayer I channeled regarding ideas and abundance. I send you every blessing as you claim this for yourself. Say the prayer out loud for maximum effectiveness.

PRAYER OF ABUNDANCE, COMFORT AND INSPIRATION

It is through the receiving of Divinely inspired ideas that wherein will raise my vibrational frequency and will attract more and more abundance into my life.

I am open to receiving the love and goodness pouring into me at every moment.

There is nothing I have to do. I AM and that is enough. Receiving the wisdom and ideas through the I AM presence sustains me and I become an attraction magnet.

In aligning my will with God's, I am sustained, wholly and completely.

As I let go of financial concerns and focus on possibilities, more possibilities open up.

As I continue to focus on gratitude and fulfilling my mission — Divine Commission — my financial needs will be met.

I remain expectant of miracles as I wait, dream, hope, and know what it means to live in the present moment, each moment of every day.

Take out your journal and write down any ideas that come to you that feel Divinely inspired. The Universe is always talking to you. Listen!

Key #37
Imagine

JOHN LENNON WOULD UNDERSTAND

After we receive an idea, it is important to nourish and nurture it. A Divine seed has been planted. Before the flower blooms, we nourish and nurture it with care and attention.

Once you receive an idea, such as writing a book, it is important to spend time seeing every aspect of this as a creation. See yourself signing copies of your book. See yourself on all the wonderful talk shows and news programs on TV. Imagine every great thing, "This or something better," is your prayer.

This is where we begin to imagine our highest good while proclaiming that we are open to a highest good, *better than we could ever imagine*! I will never forget the first time I heard those words. I took a course in angelic communication and my teacher introduced this concept. It was an introduction to learning how to communicate with the angelic realm that has blossomed into so much more.

We can imagine our ideas coming to fruition quite easily. This is an exercise that is fun and fruitful. It contains the elements of creative visualization, while allowing the Divine manifestation process to work through us. We can imagine our highest good outcome, then dare to dream and see it. When aligned with the Divine Will for our lives, it will be done and so it is.

You have the job of receiving the idea and imagining the wonderful visions and feelings that accompany the Divine manifestation of your idea. You see it concretely. If you have the idea to teach a workshop, you see yourself doing this. Imagine every detail, down to what you are wearing, saying, sharing, and most of all, imagine the great feeling of doing what you love. Feel the joy; imagine this joy. Do this often throughout the day.

Creative visualization has long been known for its effectiveness. I imagined for years that I was speaking in front of a large audience. I had severe terror around public speaking for many years, but nevertheless kept imagining how great it would feel to share my wisdom from a podium. I am now a speaker and presenter at large events. I know that while I was imagining that great dream, the Universe was working with me to help my dream come true—speaking and loving it!

What is your dream? Begin now to imagine living it with no limits. Feel and see the alignment of your highest good, dreams, and visions and forget about how to make it happen. This is pure imagination. Think, feel, and see.

EXERCISE TO IMAGINE YOUR DREAM LIFE

Find a quiet spot and close your eyes. Imagine an ideal day in your ideal life. Ask to be aligned with your highest good as you ask your Higher Self to show you a day in the life of your dreams. See yourself graduating from that program or school. Maybe you are receiving an Academy Award. Or perhaps you are tucking in your children at night, marrying your soul mate, or speaking at a convention.

Understand that this is all very personal and meaning-ful to you. This is not about singing like Mariah Carey if you know you cannot carry a tune. This is about aligning with the Universe to bring your unique gifts, talents, and experiences into your life now.

Take out your journal and write down your deepest desires, dreams, goals, and visions for your life. Spend a lot of time throughout the day imagining everything great in your life.

Key #38
Plan

EXPECT THE BEST, PLAN ON IT

The next stage in bringing your idea from the heavens down to earth is the planning stage. Before we take action, it is necessary to make a plan.

You have a great idea. You imagine your idea or dream coming true. Then you get out pen and paper and make a list of everything you need to take action on the idea that you have.

For example, if you have the idea to write a book, you figure out what you need to do ahead of time to make the process go more smoothly. You will need a computer or notebook and pen. Then, do you have a good backup system on your computer so your precious words are safe? You will need to plan out time for yourself to write. You may want to stock up on healthy snacks and herbal teas so that you are physically sustained while you write for hours at a time.

If you have an idea to take a class, you need a plan as well. The planning stage is in preparation. Think about everything you need to do ahead of time during this stage. If you want to create a website, you need a checklist of everything you need to do ahead of time before you take action. You will need a domain name, a hosting company, a name for your site, what your offerings are, and a good webmaster.

You get the point. Prepare for the best.

EXERCISE TO PLAN YOUR PRECIOUS CREATION

Find a quiet spot and get out your journal. Write down the idea that you have been dreaming about and nourishing in your imagination. Now ask your Higher Self, "What do I need to do to plan for this coming into being?"

Write down everything you can think of around your idea becoming real.

Key # 39
Action!

STOP TALKING, START DOING

Recently, around the New Year, my Higher Self began speaking louder and louder. My to-do list was a mile long. I was discerning what I needed to get done just for each day, but I was feeling a little more stress than usual. I wasn't quite sure why. I had plowed and barreled through mountains of work before. I knew eventually everything would get done, but somewhere in my inner integrity, I was not getting things done when I said I would. I had a painting I had to pick up at a local gallery and found myself moving the days in my calendar time after time. That was not like me. I honor my commitments and keep my word for my own well-being and out of respect to others.

I certainly enjoy my time with my Inner Circle. I think all of us in the Circle could gab for hours and often we do. The problem was, I was letting commitments pass, not writing this book, and not working on a new website. I was not getting a lot done.

That's when I heard that wonderful inner voice of mine say "Stop talking, start doing!" Some pretty strong energy! God or Spirit was not in the habit of telling me what to do. However, aligning my will with God's will is like a contract I made. The advice was telling me that I was not honoring my contract. So I buckled down, stopped talking, and started doing. I have been on a roll ever since. I can fit in the talking after I get my work done, or on my "break" time.

I had the idea to write this book. I received the title two years ago. I have been nurturing and imagining it that long. Then I planned everything I needed to do. Then I took action. I got my computer back-up in place. I bought a notebook just for the book. I wrote down and scheduled the best times for writing. I picked up my pen and wrote! I was doing, not just thinking about it.

This process of Divine Manifestation is co-creating with God. I take action and God meets me more than halfway. Spirit and my Higher Self, Guides, and Angels showed up to help me write this book. I am the human channel that is the vehicle and has the fingers to type these words.

You are a vehicle for Divine wisdom, ideas, and inspiration. Are you inspired with ideas? Keep thinking about them, dream about them, plan, and take action. Call on your Higher Self, Guides, Teachers, Angels, and God to help you. You have a

Celestial Dream Team. You, however, are the one on earth bringing it into reality. Are you ready to get to work?

EXERCISE FOR TAKING ACTION!
ACTIONS SPEAK LOUDER THAN WORDS

Find a quiet spot and take out your to-do list. One by one, go over the items and discern this list. Ask your Higher Self "What is the one thing on this list that is important for me to do right now?" Do it. Then ask again. Get as many things done and checked off on your list as you are guided to.

Procrastination is common for many people. It requires discipline to keep going when you feel overwhelmed or unsure about what to do next. That's why it is important to slow down and accomplish just one thing at a time. Keep your to-dos simple and you'll get more done.

Notice if you have a tendency to distract yourself; that little voice that wants to check your email or get a snack, although you are not really hungry. Notice and honor your excuses and distractions, then get back on track. Taking action will help you feel powerful. You are creating your life in every moment. Don't just dream about a great life; take the steps needed to live it.

Key #40
Your Mission

IT'S NOT IMPOSSIBLE

*I*t is helpful to create a mission statement, whether it is for personal or professional reasons. Your mission answers the *Why* of what you are doing. Why do you want to help people? What do you want them to get out of doing business with you? Why do you want to feel fulfilled every day? Your mission is as unique as you. It can be a service-oriented mission, or one to remind yourself why you are living your Soul's purpose. Your mission could simply be to feel content.

My mission is to remind people about the Divine Power within so that they can live joyfully. That is the short and sweet version. A longer version is:

My mission and passion as an Intuitive Life Purpose Coach is to help you unleash your creativity, gifts and talents, to feel and experience your team of celestial helpers and to connect you with your unique Soul 's purpose.

Your mission can include being a good listener and why that's important. It might be to help bring out laughter in life. It can be to be the best mom or dad you can be. Missions are as unique as you are.

Before I did this work professionally, I would drive to work each day and say to God, "Help me align my will with your will today. May every person I come in contact with be at peace because of my presence and how I help them." At the time, I was a receptionist and assistant property manager. I set that mission each day and could feel the difference in my life because of it. It gave me a soulful purpose.

Understand that you are living here in this physical body in this exact time in history to contribute to the world in a way that no one else can. Even if you don't think you are a saver of the world, understand that by living your joy each day, you are contributing massive amounts of high-level vibrations. When you live your joy to the fullest extent, those vibrations radiate outward from you.

Being happy helps the world. You have everything that you need to be happy. You were born knowing what you like. It is no one else's business how you live your life for your highest good. Each person has a unique life to live. You are here to express the joy of who you are. You have a purpose and everything you need to be happy. You have inner instructions on how to live your mission. You have a calling. Your calling is to live your greatest good with your greatest happiness and joy in your heart.

EXERCISE IN UNDERSTANDING YOUR MISSION

Find a quiet spot and close your eyes. Breathe consciously. Call on your Higher Self and ask, "What do I care deeply about in my life?" Do not judge what you hear; all missions in the highest good are great.

Think now about how you would spend your day if time and money were not an issue. What do you love to do? Recall what was important to you in the article writing exercise.

Now take out your journal and write a mission statement: *My Mission Is...* Write down whatever comes to you. Think of causes that are near and dear to your heart, kindness, laughter, emotional healing, physical healing, energy healing, creating beauty, or maintaining peace. There are as many missions as there are unique individuals. Keep focusing on what brings you joy and that will serve the world.

Key #41
Your Brand

YOUR ENERGY SIGNATURE

*Y*ou are unique. You have your own energy signature, like no other. For years I called myself an Angel Reader and gave readings at many events where many other angel readers were present. I never felt competition, as I have been blessed with connecting to exactly what is unique and different about me. I love helping other people find what is unique and different about them.

Along with your own unique mission, you are your own brand. Whether or not you have your own business or are thinking of having one or not, you are a brand. Some women wear perfume and are known for their signature scents. You are your own True Self. Along with that, you have experienced life like no one else on the planet. Your challenges have made you stronger, wiser, and more compassionate. You are a blend of all the wonderful energies that make you *YOU*. If you are interested in the self-help field or are already in it, realize your life has been like no one else's. You have gifts and wisdom to offer those who come to you for help. What are you known for?

EXERCISE TO TAP INTO YOUR UNIQUE BRAND OF *YOU*

Find a quiet spot and close your eyes. Let your breath guide you more deeply into this moment. Call on your Higher Self and ask, "What are my unique qualities that allow me to help people that come to *ME*?"

You were born with many of the qualities you possess. Other qualities have been hard won. Take some time to honor the wonderful qualities you have.

Take out your journal and write down one hundred qualities that make you *YOU*. One hundred seems like a lot, but you can do it. It's good to Know Your Self!

Key #42
$Your$ $Biography$

IT'S ALL ABOUT YOU

It's good to stop, take stock and honor your journey. Honoring where you have been includes a biography of who you are and what you do. Knowing who you are and what you are about on a deep level helps you swim in shark-filled waters. Whether or not you are in business or would like to start one, a biography, at the very least, brings forth a powerful inner knowingness of how capable you are. It shows you how certain you can be in sometimes uncertain times.

I help heart-centered entrepreneurs start businesses. One of the exercises I have them do is create a bio. Many say, "I don't have enough experience to create this." I show them there is more to them than they realize.

Just for fun, I am going to ask you to create the biography of your dreams. It doesn't matter if you are living those dreams yet. It's good to put into words and have in writing what you would like to accomplish, while honoring what you have accomplished thus far. This is a sample using myself:

> *Anne Deidre is an author, artist, intuitive life coach, and*
> *award–winning speaker. She enjoys cooking and gardening.*
> *Anne lives with her husband and two children.*

The idea here is that you can say you live with your cats, enjoy yoga, won an Academy Award. While I have not won any awards for speaking yet, I added that to my dream bio. You can list any schooling or training or life experiences you have had. This exercise is about getting you to think big, while realizing what you have already.

EXERCISE TO CREATE YOUR DREAM BIO
FOR YOUR IDEAL LIFE

Find a quiet spot and close your eyes. Breathe consciously and begin to think about your life being as big and wonderful as you can imagine. You have buried dreams within you; this is not the time to be practical. Go ahead! Full-out imagine what you would like to accomplish in this life.

Call on your Higher Self and ask "What are the dreams and goals in my highest good that I can add to the biography of my life?"

Take out your journal and create a biography for yourself mixing what is true now and what you would love to create. Amen. And so it is.

Key $\#$ *43*
$Your$ $Divine$ $Team$

Go, YOU!

Surrounding you in every moment are your cosmic cheerleaders. In the next several keys, I will discuss the indomitable support team surrounding you.

Since birth, you have had a guardian angel .Your guardian angel has also been described as your Higher Self or the highest aspect of your Soul. Along with that you have spirit guides, animal totem guides, and a host of many ascended beings you can call on for assistance at any time in your life.

Our lives are forever changed once we realize and tune into the wealth of assistance available to us. There is no matter too small or too big for our Divine helpers.

EXERCISE TO TUNE IN TO YOUR DIVINE SUPPORT TEAM

Find a quiet spot and close your eyes. Breathe consciously and let go of any concerns. In this moment, feel the love within and around you. Feel the peace of this moment. Feel gratitude and appreciation.

These frequencies help you become more aware of your celestial helpers. Thank your team for being with you. Tell them you are open to receiving signs from them. It's in the silence that you can hear them the best. Tell your helpers you will be more available to hear and share with them. Feel the love. It is all around you.

Key #44
Angels

I AM CALLING ALL ANGELS

I love the song *Calling All Angels* by Train. When the song came out, I thought it was a nice idea, calling on angels. Then I took a ten-week course to become an Angel Messenger Practitioner. I learned how to call on the angels. If that didn't change my life, I don't know what did. Writing my first book did that, too. That was the beginning of my connection to my Higher Self, Guardian Angel of my Soul .

God gave us free will. Angels are messengers of God. Unless we ask for their help, they cannot help us unless the situation is life-threatening. When we call on them, in an instant, they are there. You can call on legions of angels or you can simply call on angels. Whether it is a great parking spot you want or help with an important decision, angels are here to help us.

Angels have their own energy signature. Angels do not have a fluffy energy; there is great power in the angelic realm. You will recognize angelic guidance, as it is kind, loving, powerfully gentle, and strong. It is uplifting. There is no bad news with the angels. They steer us higher into the realms of the Divine, full of possibilities and potential. They do not pity us, yet they understand.

Invite the angels into your life. They are honored to serve you and will let you know that.

EXERCISE TO CONNECT WITH THE ANGELIC REALM

Find a quiet spot and close your eyes. Breathe consciously. Continue breathing comfortably. Feel peace and let go of all worry and doubt. Feel grateful for your connection to your angels. Say, "I call on my highest angels; I call on legions of angels to surround me now. I thank you for your angelic guidance on all matters near and dear to my heart. I ask that you show me signs that you are near in my daily life. I allow the grace of your presence and assistance in my life."

Now take some time to connect with this high frequency around you that is the angels. You have now given them permission to act on your behalf. Write down your experience from this exercise, your feelings and any question you have that you would like your angels to answer.

Key #45
Spirit Guides

MENTORS ON THE OTHER SIDE

*A*long with the angels, we are here with a celestial team of key players. Their best interest is to make sure they guide us with our best interest at heart, all for our highest good of course. Not all of us care about our highest good all the time and our Spirit Guides respect that.

Let me share a story about a time when I heard very clearly from my guides. It was years ago and I was in the midst of one of the more challenging times in my life. I had discovered that I could make cooling ice coffee drinks during that hot summer. I would take out my blender and whip up a chilled concoction of coffee, cream, and artificial sweetener with ice. I had a tendency to be anxious and generally ill at ease in my body. I had quit my pack-a-day cigarette smoking habit, but still had plenty of toxins running through my body.

I will never forget the voice I heard one summer day. I was about to hit high speed on my blender, anticipating an icy coffee treat. A voice said, "You are not really jittery or anxious. What is happening is that you are putting many toxic substances, like coffee, into your body. You are not anxious. You feel anxious from the adrenaline and effects of what you are eating and drinking." The voice was very matter-of-fact. While not judging me, it was not messing around. I felt at once comforted and surprised.

Since that experience, I have come to realize that without a doubt, I am guided. I also have the honor of working with clients and will hear their Spirit Guides as well. The energy signature of our guides is one of Master Teacher, very knowing, wise, and succinct. It can have an edge of cold, hard truth, which is how I distinguish this energy. It is very firm.

From what I know, many spirit guides have walked the earth and understand us on a very deep, earthly level. However, they are instructional by nature. While they understand, when you invite them in, you can be sure to be taught clearly, the highest good for your life.

EXERCISE TO CONNECT WITH YOUR SPIRIT GUIDES

Find a quiet spot and close your eyes. Breathe consciously. Feel the peace of this present moment. Call on your Spirit Guides, ask them to step forth, and just feel any shift or change in energy. Feel the strength and power of those who have gone before you. They are here for you now to guide you in all that is good. Thank your guides for their constant loving guidance and support.

Take out your journal and write down anything that comes to you around this connection with your guides. Affirm that you are willing to hear and be instructed on the highest good for your life. Write down anything you hear from your guides on any matter from your heart.

Key #46
Animal Totems

NOT JUST YOUR AVERAGE BEAR

*W*hen it comes to guidance for our lives, the good news is that there is more than we could imagine. The first time I really became aware of animals as guides was through my paintings. I had painted *Divine Mercy, Resurrection* in 2004, and when looking at it closely , I noticed faces. Now, my paintings have become known for a kind of "Where's Waldo" in them; many people see ascended masters and all sorts of faces and beings in my artwork. In that particular painting, I could see the face of a fox. Since then, I have seen the faces of many animals in my paintings.

What I know now about the animal kingdom is that each animal carries a message for us. Upon researching the fox totem (we call the messages from the animal world "totems"), I learned that Fox was about thinking creatively, expressing intensity and passion, while being adaptable to our surroundings—all perfect messages for me at that time in my life.

Animal totems can change as we evolve. Understand that you may have messages from the animal kingdom that can assist you on your journey. Perhaps you see some ducks in a pond and later you see another sign of ducks. Watch for sequences with the animals you see. Seeing or hearing or reading about a particular animal could be a sign that you are receiving a wonderful message. You can search the Internet for animal totems or meanings to find out more.

EXERCISE TO CONNECT WITH YOUR POWER ANIMAL

Find a quiet spot and close your eyes. Breathe consciously. In the quiet and solitude you are experiencing, ask for the highest good animal to come through now and offer a message. This is a very intuitive exercise.

When you ask for an animal to connect with you, you will receive one. Hear the name of the type of animal in your intuition. Write down what you have been given.

Ask if there is any other animal from the animal kingdom that would like to come through now with a message. Write down what you get. You can research your animal through Ted Andrew's book, _Animal Speak,_ or an internet search. Enjoy your message from your animal friend and guide.

Key #47
Herbs and Flowers

TIPTOE THROUGH THE TULIPS
AND BE HEALED

*I*n terms of health, wealth, and happiness, understand that we have a bounty of earth gifts near to us from which we can reap many benefits. For the longest time, I imagined having a garden filled with herbs and a yard filled with flowers. My dear father, who has since passed away, gave me a subscription to *Better Homes and Gardens* magazine, hoping that I would enjoy the bounty of the land as he had throughout his life.

My home always needed some improvements and I thank him for his guidance with that. My father was a hardworking business-man, gardener, and keeper of the earth. Not a weekend went by without my father mowing the lawn, stacking wood, filling whiskey-barrel planters with flowers, planting vegetables, and taking care of the earth.

In terms of healing and health, the land provides much. You can research the many benefits of herbs such as basil, rosemary, thyme, and oregano. Flowers are also beneficial and carry a high vibration. In addition to having flowers in your yard or home, there are flower essences you can take to harmonize your mind, body, and spirit connection. As always, check with your doctor. Understand that holistic health is here and it is time to use the rich benefits of the plant world.

EXERCISE TO CONNECT WITH
THE BOUNTY OF MOTHER NATURE

Find a quiet spot and feel the peace of this moment. Bring your awareness to this present moment. Mother Nature is alive. All in the natural world are here to serve your highest good and allow healthy living.

Bring plants into your home environment; they will oxygenate the air. Herbs and flowers will also assist in providing well-being and health. You can add many herbs to your cooking.

The rose is one of the highest vibrations on the planet. You can find good quality rose oil, plant a rose bush, or enjoy roses in a vase on your table. Fill your home and environment with herbs and flowers and you will notice the difference.

Key # 48
Masters of Light

ABOVE AND BEYOND, LET THERE BE LIGHT

Writing my first book was such a magical experience and so not what was usual for me that I found myself asking "Who wrote this book?" It was a completely new experience for me to just have information flow through me with such ease and grace and wisdom. I knew that I connected with my Higher Self, that part of me that was connected to Spirit like an angel on my shoulder.

I also recognize that I had other help with that first book. I received quotes from Jesus and an understanding of Buddha that can be described as miraculous.

I now know that my commitment to the Light has brought in this help. I am an Adept Initiate with the Modern Mystery School. I am initiated into the Universal Brother and Sisterhood of Light. I am in agreement and committed to work with the Hierarchy of Light. *What does all that mean?* you might ask. Good question. I will answer from my heart.

When I went through my debilitating depression and anxiety, I prayed. When I experienced heartache and lost jobs, I prayed. I prayed and asked for help my whole life — well, from age 26 or so — when I realized I had run out of road. I prayed to the God of my understanding.

When I refer to the Masters of Light, I am talking about working with a group of Masterful Beings who understand and teach and advise me on the highest level. These Spiritual Masters encourage us to become self-realized in our own spiritual mastery. They encourage us to realize and live our full potential.

These last several keys have been about guides and guidance. I invite you to call on the Masters of Light. There are too many to mention here, but know they have the depth of wisdom, knowledge, and help for you that is above and beyond this earthly plane. Talk about friends in high places!

EXERCISE TO CONNECT WITH THE MASTERS OF LIGHT

Find a quiet spot and close your eyes. Breathe consciously, notice your breath, and stay present to it. In this feeling of deep peace, call on the Masters of Light.

You can feel the deep peace of connection, as they are here for you. Tell them you are open to their teachings for your life on the highest spiritual level. Thank them for their guidance, wisdom, and assistance. For a life filled with purpose, the Masters will advise and guide you in every way.

Take out your journal and write about any guidance that you receive from the Masters of Light.

Key #49

$Cosmic$ $Consciousness$

STARRY, STARRY NIGHT

I wonder if Vincent Van Gogh would have felt less traumatized as an artist if he had been aware that he was connecting to the Universe when he was painting. As an artist of over 20 years, I certainly was not aware of that. I have had people say to me, "You'll make money in your art when you are dead." I have painted and just thrown my work in a pile, thinking nothing about what I had just done.

What I realize now is that we have a connection to Cosmic Consciousness. Why is this important? There is an overwhelming peace and feeling of well-being when we connect to All That Is. It doesn't take a guru or a Master to connect to God and the Divine Consciousness, or to connect to the field of all potential and possibilities as contained in the field of Cosmic Consciousness. It takes a sincere seeker, a spiritual aspirant. It is about you who know, who long to meet God face to face, and to receive all the bounty and Divine Providence from that encounter.

Upon meeting the Divine, in the field of All That Is, you will remember who you are. You will remember that nothing was ever kept from you regarding your well-being. You will remember that you have access to other worlds and dimensions that can help you with your life now. You will remember that while on Earth, time is finite, but in the spiritual world, there are no limits. Freedom and truth reign supreme. You remember that you are a spiritual being in a physical world and that you can move mountains.

EXERCISE TO CONNECT WITH COSMIC CONSCIOUSNESS

Find a quiet spot and close your eyes. Breathe consciously and focus on your breath. Here and now, you have access to All That Is. In all time, space, and dimensions, there are no veils. There is nothing you cannot know if it is to serve your highest good.

Imagine a night sky filled with stars. See the space between the stars. See the stars glow and glisten. In the vision of this starry sky, ask for Spirit to guide you to the answers you are seeking. You are a child of God, worthy of receiving all the answers to your questions.

Take out your journal and ask for the answers you are seeking. Stay open to receive the guidance from the Cosmos, from Spirit. It is your birthright to know joy and receive answers. Write down what you receive from this place of Cosmic Consciousness.

Key #50
Art

TAKE IT SERIOUSLY

When I went to college, I spent some time figuring out what it is that I "wanted to do" with my life. I remember considering majoring in Political Science, as I got an A in the class and my parents would surely approve. I was happy I had a path. Although I knew Poli Sci was not what I really wanted, it was something. My best friend in college asked me to go to her Art History class with her, saying, "I think you'll like it." I was sold. I loved everything about the class. Dim lighting, art projected on the screen, larger than life. No dull lectures. I was in. I became a new Art History major.

My parents took the news well. Just "major in something" was the Liberal Arts motto back then. Art history was not without challenges, and involved memorizing hundreds of paintings, dates, and artists, as well as lots of "compare and contrast." I finally received my Bachelor of Arts in Art History. After decades in business jobs, do you think I ever questioned my Art History major? You betcha! I questioned my decision until 2004, when I heard my intuition tell me to pull out my paintings. I was going to write a book about them—my own art history, if you will. How perfect!

So why is art in this book? Remember our discussion of the left and right brain I mentioned in the beginning? Well, it seems like those cave men had something going on there with their ancient cave drawings. The left brain is the home of logic, practicality, language, and order. The right brain houses creativity and intuition—which is accessed through art.

I created a set of oracle cards from my paintings and then channeled the messages. I am a highly intuitive channel and I do professional intuitive coaching. This ability has been nurtured through years of study with the history of art and then creating art myself. Do you need to study art or paint to be highly intuitive? No, there are many other means and I have talked about them in the other keys. I have to mention art to be complete here. Art has been a floodgate and means for me to open to the higher realms. It is there for you, too.

EXERCISE TO CONNECT WITH YOUR INNER ARTIST

We discussed in Key #3 how to connect to your inner artist with Intuitive Painting. Along with that, I want to encourage you to visit an art museum or gallery near you.

Look around you with an artist's eye and take photos as guided. Photography is a wonderful art form as well. You don't need expensive equipment; just use the camera on your phone, if you have one. Begin to notice the beauty around you. See, feel, and connect with this beauty. Draw, paint, or take photos of what inspires you.

Key #51
Muscle Testing

STRENGTH CAN BE FELT

As I've said before, everything is energy. Every thought, every feeling, the food we eat, and the music we listen to. In your *Extreme Intuitive Makeover,* you realize that what you eat, listen to, or put into your body affects you. If you want to maintain the energy of health, wealth, and happiness, it helps to maintain a vibration that matches those things.

There are simple ways to test energy. To see what kind of energy I am ingesting or taking in musically or reading, I have found the following exercise to be helpful.

EXERCISE FOR TESTING STRONG OR WEAK ENERGY

You will need a partner for this exercise.

Stand and extend your right arm out horizontally from your shoulder. With your left hand, hold the item you want to test—it could be a food, a book, or CD. Hold the item close to your heart with your left hand, while your right arm is extended out from your shoulder.

Think about the energy of what you are holding as your partner begins to push down on your right arm. If your arm goes down easily, what you are holding has weak energy. If you are able to keep your arm strong, the item has strong energy. Understand that weak energy will affect you. If you listen to music or eat food with a weaker vibration, it will affect you. Know this; it is good to make choices out of wisdom.

Key #52
Enlightenment

ME? ENLIGHTENED?

I thought that only the most ascended beings could claim enlightenment. What is enlightenment really about? From my understanding, we are already connected to God through our Spirit. Our souls are learning lessons so that we can remember who we are. Light is information. When we claim enlightenment, we claim we have received and integrated all the information from God and there is nothing left to say. We can be in 100-percent service.

Enlightenment is attainable. For those of us who feel less than enlightened, know this: Stay open. Keep aligning your will with Divine Will. Allow the Light to transform you. Light is wisdom.

In our human experience, we have a lot to transform within us. The Light will help us. All the pain, suffering, heartache, and resentments are not of the Light. Intend that the Light work through you. Understand that there is holy knowledge and wisdom that can turn on the light in the darkest places.

Start a new day and a new dawn, understanding that the pain of yesterday does not have to rule today. Ask for the Light to shine in all the dark places of your heart and life.

EXERCISE TO CONNECT WITH YOUR ENLIGHTENED SELF

Find a quiet spot and close your eyes. Breathe consciously as you connect to your True Self.

You are Light. You are Love. You are a Radiant Being. There is no limitation to what you can do and offer the world. Allow yourself to feel the expansiveness of your great being. Imagine knowing the highest good answer for every question that you ask, because you do.

Imagine your whole body filled with light energy. Feel this energy as white-gold light coming down from the heavens through the top of your head, down through your spine, and out the bottoms of your feet.

Allow any dense energy to leave you. Know and go with this Light into the core of the earth. Mother Earth can transmute this energy. Gather this white-gold light, along with the grounded green-gold energy of Earth, and pull it up through your feet. Feel the Light travel up your spine and out the top of your head back to the heavens. Feel every cell of your body renewed with this green, gold, and white healing light.

Key #53
The Ones We Love

NO SPIRITUAL DOORMATS HERE

I believe that Love can heal and transform the planet and all beings. I also know that with free will, we can feel as though we are banging our heads against the wall with friends and family. I have discussed earlier how important it is to speak from our Communication Wealth Center with Love. The words spoken from our hearts create no harm.

It is true that we can outgrow friends and feel distant from our families. Understand that we are evolving all the time. Marriages dissolve. People grow apart. In this new age, keep in mind that now we can maintain the vibration of relationships in truth only. Veils are being lifted. If you have an issue with someone, you owe it to your own integrity and to them to discuss it with the most kind and loving energy that you can.

We are all choosing our many "mansions in heaven" and we are not all choosing the same things. Like will continue to attract like, meaning that whatever vibration you are radiating will show up in your life. I say no spiritual doormats here, because we are now empowered to speak our truth with love. This means that those who have had trouble hearing us or can no longer *not* hear us, will make choices that reflect our power of choice to live in harmony, peace, and cooperation.

EXERCISE TO SILENTLY COMMUNICATE TO THOSE WE LOVE

Find a quiet spot and close your eyes. Breathe consciously. Imagine someone with whom you are in conflict. Ask your Higher Self and the other person's Higher Self to come forth.

Begin to talk about whatever you are having difficulty with. Express yourself to this person. Ask for the angels to act on your behalf to resolve this situation and release it to the Light.

Whatever challenge is between you and this person, ask to be free from turmoil with it. Forgive yourself and the other person. Leave it in God's hands. Know that by expressing and releasing, you have your celestial team helping you to a new understanding.

Key #54
Smile...

...THOUGH YOUR HEART IS BREAKING

That's a nice line from a song I heard in my intuition and I ask, *Really, do I have to do that?* I meditated a few months ago, around the time I described in Key #29. I had heard in my intuition that I should take care of myself, my home, and my children, rather than tend to my to-do list. During the meditation, I heard in my intuition, "Smile more, laugh more, and enjoy yourself." *People! I have work to do on the Earth! Are you saying the laundry and my pearly whites are much more important than everything else I have to do?*

"Yes," I heard. "Smile."

Once I heard that, of course, the word *smile* came up repeatedly. It was the Universe's way of showing me its wonderful signs. So smile it is!

When I was asking Spirit about the closing of this book, guess what I heard? "Talk about Smiling."

OK. I am your dutiful servant. Smile it is. I am smiling as I write this. What is it about smiling that matters with our health, our wealth, or our happiness? I'm hearing that there is an inner smile from our hearts. The definition of smile includes the words "regarded with favor."

I am reminded that God smiles at us, as we are highly regarded with favor. I am reminded of how light and joyful we can be if we only let go of the denseness we grasp and carry. I am reminded that we are here to travel lightly, with a smile. It is indeed possible to uplift someone in a moment when we smile.

There are so many so-called reasons not to smile. It is easy to get bogged down with the rationalization of all of our problems. At times, to smile is to defy gravity. When we force a smile, it can also make us feel better instantly. It defies logic in many ways, yet feels uplifting and true all at once.

EXERCISE FOR HAPPINESS

Smile!

Key #55
Christ Consciousness

HERE, NOW, AND FOREVER

As I conclude the chapter in my life of writing this book, I know that my experience with the Christ Consciousness is something I need to put into words. My first book was about connecting to a part of me I had never fully realized. I pray that the attempt to put the enormity of this experience into writing will do it justice.

When teachers let me know I was not quite good enough, bosses let me go from jobs, and boyfriends broke up with me, it became very easy for me to slide into a spiral of self-rejection and self-destruction. I did and I did it well, so well that I almost had a complete nervous breakdown. I now call it "my dark night of the soul." I had taken my free will and run myself into the ground. You name it, I did it. It got me nowhere, but not fast enough. I slow-burned for a long time, until the jig was up. I became catatonic. I could not feel any joy, could not sleep or eat. I could barely care for myself or my children. The light was out.

I was "with it" enough to know I was in deep trouble. My doctor just kept prescribing more medicine, lethal doses and combinations of anti-depressive medications and anxiety medications. So many bottles they gave me. I could have taken a handful and ended it all. I thought about it. I was in enormous pain. Thank God I thought about my children. I could not see the light, but some faint memory of faith was there.

After a month of barely moving, I went to the health food store. My life was at stake and I knew it. I picked up a free magazine. One of the articles was "Christ Consciousness — Receiving the Divine."

This story has a happy ending. I ordered the Kriya Yoga DVD and book and practiced it. I meditated and I received the Christ Consciousness the book had promised. Thank you, Norman Paulsen, and thank you, Yogananda, for bringing such a powerful spiritual tool to this world.

I have not looked back. I continue to grow and learn and experience life from a new level. My heart and my consciousness, and your heart and your consciousness — matter. Know there is so much Divine potential for you to experience here and now. I pray these words have been a blessing to you.

Exercise to Connect With The Christ Consciousness

Understand that this is not a religion. We are all beings of consciousness. Call on the Christed energy to be with you. Open your heart to receive the love here for you now. Enjoy your life as a being who is here to live in joy, peace, love, and fulfillment. Know that you are love and here to express love.

I see you as the great eternal being that you are. You are whole, you are healed, and you are eternally wealthy and happy beyond measure. I honor you. May you be blessed and always know who you are and enjoy every step of the way of your journey. You are not alone. You are loved. You are here to contribute in a way that is like no other. I see you. I know who you are. Namaste. Joy.

Afterword

May the keys in this book bless you. May you feel fulfilled from the inside out—with yourself and your life. I have included some articles as samples to show you how to write a self-help article if you aspire to do so.

Please visit my website at www.annedeidre.com for information on my personal sessions, coaching, teleseminars, and other services. You'll also be able to receive your complimentary copy of *Your Prosperous Life Kit,* which includes a special report on your life's purpose and an angel art print, and more.

Sample Article

KINDNESS MATTERS
BY ANNE DEIDRE

We all have the choice to be kind in every moment of every day. Kindness matters, as the love, mercy, and compassion we demonstrate to each other create an everlasting, eternal bond. My beloved father passed away on April 15, 2001. The lesson of kindness he taught me is timeless. The passing of my father was the single most awakening moment in my life. I had never known such deep devastation and loss. However, it was at his funeral and the many cards sent to me afterward that resounded what I knew about his life, it was his kindness that people remembered.

Every relationship we have holds an opportunity for growth, at the very least. As people come and go in our lives, it is important to remember that within each encounter is an opportunity for holiness. We are often challenged by our relationships with people. We all experience stress and pressure. Kindness is a choice. Every day, we may be confronted by negativity at work and in our personal relationships. A natural reaction may be to lash out because of our own stress. God gave us free will. With that said, if we take the time to see someone else's point of view, we begin to develop compassion. A good rule of thumb may be to wait 24 hours before we respond to a perceived unkindness from others.

The way we respond to people in our lives matters on so many levels. The easy way out is to fight fire with fire. Again with free will, this is a choice. We all have the opportunity to take the higher road and not respond in anger. Only love is real. We are all spiritual beings in a physical world. We all have experienced drama in our lives. We often connect with each other through drama, which contains anger, jealousy, and resentment. This is may be conscious or unconscious. As Dr. Barbara De Angelis so eloquently writes in her incredibly transformational book *How did I Get Here?*, there may be a "loving conspiracy" in your life. She writes that is "what happens when consciously or unconsciously, those closest to us undermine our efforts to grow or change."

Sometimes we may need to let go of people in our lives with love. Archangel Michael can help us cut the cords with people with whom we have connected through the lower energies of anger, jealousy, resentment—all that is not love. Ask him to remove all cords from you that are not of love. These lower energy cords drain you. Remember that your Higher Self is your true reality. The cords of love through which we connect with each other will remain in eternity. Be kind in every moment, as you will create an everlasting bond with everyone, in every situation. That is Heaven on Earth.

BELOW IS AN ARTICLE USING "THE FORMULA" I PRESENTED IN KEY #5

HOW TO LIVE FEARLESSLY IN A FEAR-FILLED WORLD

*I*n *A Course in Miracles,* there is a saying that "Nothing Real Can Be Threatened." This brings a tremendous amount of peace to me during challenging times.

The ability to be certain through times of uncertainty means that whatever I am facing, I am certain that the Divine plan for me is being followed. How do we trust that what is happening in the moment is for our highest good? How do we know that we are always OK? How do we trust that if we lose our job or our partner leaves us that we won't go into despair, to stay there, to fall and not get up? One of my favorite sayings is from the Zen belief system: "Fall down six times, get up seven."

Part of my Soul's journey has been to learn to experience peace no matter what I am facing. I want my life to be free of emotional pain. I believe that this is possible.

Here are five ways to help you cope with any challenge that you are facing, when you feel as though you are waiting for the other shoe to drop. Try these pointers:

1. Value Every Experience

Understand that there is always a silver lining during negative times and events. Have the awareness that it is not what happens, but rather our perception of what is happening that is the root of our suffering. It is easy to value positive experiences, but how about the negative ones? A so-called negative experience could be that door closing before the next one opens. Find the gift in the negative experience. Ask yourself "What have I learned from this?" and you will be on your way to acceptance, trust and peace.

2. Remember that "Nothing Real Can Be Threatened" from *A Course in Miracles*

This to me is the ultimate in trust. Meditating on this statement can bring relief and peace. What does "Nothing Real Can Be Threatened" mean? If it is a job you are losing, know that no matter what is "taken away" on the outside, the source of your abundance is on the inside. No matter what you do for work, you can offer gifts of kindness, love, and service wherever you are.

Being a mystic means working for the Light, for God. This is limitless and has no boundaries. In a love relationship, "Nothing Real Can Be Threatened." Real love lasts; it is eternal. Feel the love that is inside of you, connected to God, Source energy and offer love. Remember love is a journey, not a destination.

3. QUESTION FALSE BELIEFS

This can take a little work, but is very freeing. Begin to notice your thoughts. What are you telling yourself? The thoughts of the ego are subtle and damaging. Are you scaring yourself, telling yourself that you will never win, have love, or succeed? Our thoughts are either based on fear or love. Fear thoughts are an illusion, because only love is real.

Notice your thoughts, question them. Replace fear-filled thoughts with positive, loving ones. This will bring a sense of calm and peace.

4. UNDERSTAND THAT SELF-SABOTAGE HAPPENS AND CAN BE CLEARED

In my Soul 's journey, I have worked on clearing my subconscious beliefs. Wherever you go, there you are. I believe that our past life experiences are in our subconscious and without meaning to, we can be creating the same negative experiences over and over. This is because we are meant to heal these false beliefs. Know that there is help and that these beliefs can be cleared at the root. You can experience happiness, abundance and freedom in your life.

5. BE PATIENT, KIND, GENTLE, AND FORGIVING WITH YOURSELF

Living fearlessly can be the ultimate in living a joy-filled life. It transcends the world. Make every day an adventure in being kind to yourself. If you notice that you are "beating yourself up," forgive yourself. Tell yourself that you are doing the best you can and let yourself off the hook.

Treating ourselves in this way helps us to be able to treat others with kindness as well, bringing Heaven on Earth.

Article Source: http://EzineArticles.com/?expert=Anne_Deidre_Smith